A Layman Looks at the Names of J E S U S

A Layman Looks at THE Names OF Jesus

JOHN H. TIMMERMAN

Tyndale House
Publishers, Inc.
Wheaton, Illinois

Unless otherwise noted, all Scripture quotations are
taken from the Revised Standard Version.

First printing, October 1985
Library of Congress Catalog Card Number 85-51178
ISBN 0-8423-2110-1, paper

To Patricia Lynn,
who so loves that everything
becomes more and more itself,

and to George and Nancy Buth
and the members of the
Men's Support Fellowship,

without whose prayers,
encouragement, and insights
this book wouldn't be possible.

CONTENTS

ONE
GIFT

A familiar song of the church proclaims: "His name above
all names shall stand. . . . Blessed be the name." The song
is a ringing affirmation of the name of our Lord and
Savior—a name at which, someday, every knee shall bow
and every tongue confess that Jesus is Lord. Indeed, says
Acts 4:12, "There is no other name under heaven given
among men by which we must be saved."

But what mysterious, unique quality about the name of
Jesus is so powerful? Is the phrase, "In Jesus' Name," just
a closing to our prayers? Or is there something deeper
here that we must plumb for meaning?

Surely power and glory are called forth by the name of
Jesus. Imagine yourself in a vast court into which are
ushered first the great presidents of our nation. What
thunderous applause would greet Washington, Jefferson,
or Lincoln as the name of each is announced and he
walks the aisle. Then imagine, if you will, the great
authors, scientists, preachers, and prophets—all entering
to raptures of applause. Think of the reception awaiting
kings and queens. Finally, imagine the shining radiance
that bathes the court as Jesus walks through the gate.
Applause? Not very likely. As he enters, one can only

imagine that all those assembled bend the knee as if a wave swept the room. Only worship will do when the King of Kings appears.

In a very real sense, all the good gifts the other guests represent—the skills, accomplishments, and authority— are possible only by the gift of grace from Jesus. "Every good endowment and every perfect gift is from above," writes James (James 1:17).

Since he is the giver of all good gifts, Jesus deserves our thanks in thunders of praise. But above all, he deserves our worship because he himself is the greatest gift God ever gave to the world (John 4:10). No gift, however, has any value *unless* it is received. Many of us can recall gifts we refused. Perhaps a grandparent wanted to tuck a few dollars in our hand. Perhaps a neighbor or friend wanted to do a kindness for us, but we felt we didn't want to burden them. Jesus has already borne *our* burdens; all the cares we cast on him have already been received by his body on the cross. In turn, he offers us free gifts—power, healing, joy, life everlasting—all in his name.

Sometimes, when face-to-face with the priceless gift we have received, we feel compelled to give some of our own. Christmas, the celebration of God's gift to us, is, after all, remembered by an exchange of gifts that represents our love from Jesus given to others. Yet what gift can we bring the great Gift-Giver? Have we frankincense, myrrh, or gold? Would even these suffice for the priceless gift of eternal life? Christina Rossetti answered the question in her simple poem "Christmas Carol":

What can I give him,
  Poor as I am?
If I were a shepherd
  I would bring a lamb,
If I were a wise man
  I would do my part,

```
      KFC    E720089
    1617 RESEARCH PARK DRIVE
DAVIS,    CA   95616
      530-756-2400
```

149 Week No. 41 Period # 11
04/10/08   6:23 pm
SERVER ROSA

Order #   183

Drive Thru

```
1 BLT W/ TR FILET            4.15
1 NO DRESSING                0.00
            Sub Total        4.15
                   Tax       0.32
```

Total   4.47

Tendered   4.47

Change   0.00

Please take a brief survey about this visit and you could be one of our weekly $1,000 winners.

For your chance to win call

1-888-731-9645

or visit

www.opinionport.com/yum

Limit 1 entry every 6 weeks.

Díganos en español. ¿Cómo le estamos atendiendo a usted?

$1,000 AWARDED WEEKLY

SAY & PLAY FOR $1,000!

Please take a brief survey about this visit and you could be one of our weekly $1,000 winners.

For your chance to win call

1-888-731-9645

or visit

www.opinionport.com/yum

Limit 1 entry every 6 weeks.

Yet what can I give him,
  Give my heart.

My hope is that the following meditations will help us better understand God's gift to us and will kindle in us the desire to offer our hearts in return.

But more than this, I hope we will see Jesus as the Lord Immanuel, the one who is among us. For the names of Jesus are not mysterious. When Scripture refers to Jesus as the Rock, the Good Shepherd, or the Living Water, it reveals to us certain things about his nature. What does Scripture mean when it calls Jesus *our* rock? What does it mean when it says Jesus is *our* shepherd—especially for those of us who have seldom even seen a sheep? The names of Jesus can still speak to us today with all the authority, force, and power they had when Scripture was written.

REVELATION 15:3, 4

And they sing the song of Moses, the servant of God,
and the song of the Lamb, saying,
"Great and wonderful are thy deeds,
O Lord God the Almighty!
Just and true are thy ways,
O King of the ages!
Who shall not fear and glorify thy name,
O Lord?
For thou alone art holy."

PRAYER

Jesus, before your name I bow in adoration,
for yours is the honor, the power, and the glory,
forevermore.
Open my heart to receive you, precious Gift,
more clearly, more dearly,
day by day.

TWO
JESUS

What's in a name?

A name does more than simply identify one among many. Often a name evokes the image of a person, as well as events, hopes, and joys tied to that person. When we call to mind, for example, the name of a childhood friend, suddenly a whole time filled with meaning is called forth in our memory.

What's in a name? At the name of Jesus, our faith, hope, salvation, and expectation of eternal life are called forth in our thoughts.

Jesus, however, was not such an unusual name in scriptural times. In the Old Testament, Hebrew names such as Joshua, Jehoshua, and Jeshua are simply linguistic variations of Jesus. There were high priests, Bible historians, and commoners called Jesus. One of the books of the Apocrypha, Ecclesiasticus, was written by one Jesus, son of Sirach.

In the New Testament, the name is also a frequent appellation. In fact, there is reasonable evidence that Barabbas's first name was Jesus, a fact that dramatically highlights Pilate's question: "Which would you like me to release to you—Jesus Bar-Abbas, or Jesus called Messiah?" (Matt. 27:17, NEB).

While the name itself is fairly common, meaning "God's salvation," or "God is my help," the person of Jesus the Messiah is unique, for here *in fact* is God's salvation. The name at once emphasizes Jesus' commonness—he is born the Son of Man, a man among men—and Jesus' uniqueness. *This* man Jesus is born to redeem man to eternal life.

The name Jesus was appointed by God for his Son and was so announced by angelic messengers before his birth: "She will bear a son, and you shall call his name Jesus, for he will save his people from their sins" (Matt. 1:21).

This Jesus is the One who has been looked for, the One who finally comes to fulfill prophecy and expectation, the One whose birth is announced with joy and the acclamation of angels. This Jesus comes as the fulfillment of certain names known to expectant people for centuries: the Rock, the Living Water, the Bread of Life, the Good Shepherd. And he comes as the bearer of certain titles— equally familiar—draped about his human shoulders with royal, divine significance: the Messiah, the High Priest, the King, the Son of Man and Son of God.

William Barclay, the great theologian who has studied the life and work of Jesus in keen detail, says in *Jesus as They Saw Him* (Grand Rapids, Mich.: Eerdmans, 1978):

It is no accident that our Lord was called by the name Jesus. That name sums up the things which he came into the world to do and which only he can do. He came to be the divine Rescuer who alone can deliver men from the consequences and from the grip of sin; he came to be the divine Physician who alone can bring healing to the bodies and souls of men.

The Holy Scripture is a resonant proclamation of that great name, Jesus, and the promises it carries for his people.

In his name is power. "If you ask anything in my

name," Jesus says to his disciples and to us, "I will do it" (John 14:14).

In his name is healing. Demons are cast out in Jesus' name. The lame run with joy, the blind see. And, in the greatest healing, the dead in Christ are raised to eternal life (John 10:28).

In his name is joy. "These things I have spoken to you," says Jesus, "that my joy may be in you" (John 15:11). Jesus can banish all sorrow, all darkness, if only we ask.

In his name is remission of sins. "Repentance and forgiveness of sins," says Jesus, "should be preached in [Christ's] name to all nations" (Luke 24:47).

In his name there is new life. "These are written that you may believe that Jesus is the Christ, the Son of God, and that believing you may have life in his name" (John 20:31).

In his name is praise. Jesus has come "in order that the Gentiles might glorify God for his mercy" (Rom. 15:9).

Surely there is promise in the name of Jesus—the very promise of God himself.

2 THESSALONIANS 3:5
May the Lord direct your hearts to the love
of God and to the steadfastness of Christ.

PRAYER
O Lord, at all times of beginning you are there,
as you were at the first beginning.
In you all things begin and end,
and I commit this start to you
so that I may also end in you.

THREE
I AM

Since the godhood of Jesus is the key theme of the New
Testament, John starts his gospel with some ringing
affirmations. "In the beginning was the Word"—Jesus is
eternal. "And the Word was with God"—Jesus is his own
distinct, divine being from all eternity, since to be *with*
someone necessitates that you be someone yourself. "And
the Word was God"—Jesus fully shares in godhood with
the Father and the Holy Spirit (John 1:1).

To begin with Jesus, then, one must begin with God.
Jesus, as the Son of God, partakes of all the activities and
attributes of his Father. This means, for example, that
Jesus fully participated in the great act of Creation. Some
theologians say he did this as the "effective power," the
one who carried out the Father's commands.

That Jesus is God also means that he fully participates
in all of God's claims about his own divinity. Jesus, like
God, is everlasting, all-powerful, all-knowing, and always
present. As the Lord God named himself to Moses, so
Jesus is named.

Moses trod the hillsides and plains of Midian, tending
the herds of his father-in-law Jethro. He was restless in
the land, and as a sign of his restlessness, he named his

firstborn son Gershom, saying, "I have been a sojourner in a foreign land" (Exod. 2:22). Moses could not return to his people in Egypt because he had slain an Egyptian guard and had fled from Pharaoh. Now Pharaoh has died, and God himself has laid a plan for Moses to return—this time to lead all of God's people out of bondage. But with what authority could Moses dare face the magnificence of the new Pharaoh and demand the release of his people? Under whose authority could Moses come to the people as their leader?

Under *this* authority, responded God: "I Am Who I Am. . . . Say this to the people of Israel, 'I Am has sent me to you.' " (Exod. 3:14). The identification is an interesting one, particularly when—as here—we realize that it also describes Jesus. By naming himself I Am Who I Am, God reveals certain things about himself.

First, God is eternal. The Hebrew word for I Am is in an indefinite tense meaning, at once, I was, I am, and I shall always be. Thus, God says, I am the eternal One, the One who is both above all time and in all time.

Second, God is complete in himself. Throughout time, he does not change. He will always be who he is, never diminished in all of time's turning.

Third, God does not have to be known by reference to anything other than himself. God is the source of all being, of all life. Therefore it is sufficient to simply say I Am Who I Am. I am the Creator. I am the Provider. I am the Redeemer. These qualities might be named additionally, but they are all already contained within the majestic, almighty nature of the one who is God.

Fourth, God keeps part of his nature hidden from man. "For as the heavens are higher than the earth, so are my ways higher than your ways," the Lord declares (Isa. 55:9). We cannot know all there is to know about God. In naming himself, God discloses only as much about himself as Moses is able to know—and as much as he needs to know. It is sufficient to obey the voice of the

Lord according to his revealed will. We cannot presume to know God wholly. It is enough that God will be God himself to us.

JOHN 8:58

Jesus said to them, "Truly, truly, I say to you, before Abraham was, I Am."

PRAYER

Lord of all eternity, our great I Am,
who was before all things, who is now,
and who shall be forever,
thank you for your great, inexpressible power
which reaches from all time
to hold fast this time.
Thank you for your love now, in this place,
at this time.

FOUR
IMAGE OF
THE INVISIBLE GOD

While God identified himself in linguistic claims such as his revelation to Moses, or by direct address such as the commandments, he most commonly revealed himself to people in the Old Testament through images they could readily visualize. God adapted his greatness to the limited understanding of man. Among theologians this method is known as anthropomorphic language, which means quite simply that God reveals himself in human terms.

Examples abound in Scripture. The following will demonstrate some of the figures of speech God used to show his nature to man.

Nostrils of God. The first sin must have been a terrible thing to God—this sudden dark mark on the pure beauty of his new creation. Often in the Old Testament, the anger of God at man's sin is revealed in the image of smoking nostrils (2 Sam. 22:9; Job 4:9; Job 41:20; Ps. 18:8).

Does this mean God's nostrils literally steamed with smoke? It is preferable to say God uses this figure of speech to reveal to man the extent of his anger; that is, if God were a man, his nostrils would seem to smoke with wrath because his anger is as hot as a fire. God accommodates himself to our understanding so we can comprehend how terribly sin grieves him.

Arm of God. The Israelites prized military prowess, which was then demonstrated in a mighty arm. To them, such strength represented victory over threatening enemies and security in their homeland. When God says to Job, "Have you an arm like God, and can you thunder with a voice like his?" (Job 40:9), he is not pointing out that he has firm biceps but that he has *omnipotence—* complete power. No human arm is like the Lord's, but God uses this term to reveal to man's understanding his great and glorious power.

In other sections of the Old Testament, the arm of the Lord also refers to God's mercy (Ps. 77:15), his protection (Isa. 33:2), his ruling power (Ezek. 20:33; Isa. 40:10), his saving power (Exod. 6:6; Isa. 59:16), and his glory (Isa. 63:12).

Hand of God. The human hand expresses a wide range of emotions: the clenched fist shows either strength or anger, the outstretched palm expresses an offering, hands held back tight to the body communicate rejection.

Similarly, Scripture conveys a variety of God's relations to his people through figures of speech involving the hand. When the psalmist Asaph cries out in Psalm 74:11, "Why dost thou hold back thy hand, why dost thou keep thy right hand in thy bosom?" he feels deserted by God to his enemies. But in other psalms, such as 21:8, the writer proclaims that God will extend his hand to seek out his enemies. When God declares in Isaiah 65:2 that he has spread out his hands to his people, the figure indicates that he has extended mercy to them (see also Prov. 1:24). In Exodus 15:6, God's right hand is spoken of as a figure of power.

We see here, then, just three of many examples. In each instance, God discloses himself to his people in terms they can understand. Just as we gain knowledge of God by these figures in the Old Testament, so, too, we gain knowledge of him through the person of Jesus. The One who is at once our Savior and our most high Lord, the image of God the Father, is revealed to us in terms we can understand and cherish. Here God's unlimited grace is demonstrated: He puts his majesty, his power, his greatness in human form, in terms our limited understanding can readily apprehend.

COLOSSIANS 1:15
He is the image of the invisible God, the
first-born of all creation.

PRAYER
What matchless grace,
what unbounded love,
that you should step from your majesty
in heaven
and humble yourself as a man
on earth
To make yourself known—clearly and directly,
to me.
For this I thank you.

FIVE
ROCK:
PROTECTOR

Imagine yourself in a vast, shimmering desert that reaches
unbroken in a white wave to the horizon. Many miles
behind, you left the last oasis where you knelt to drink
brackish water in the flitting shade of palm trees.

In the desert, all things seem to slide and lose shape. In
the heat, which pierces like a sword, the sands seem to
heave and roll like acres of baking bread. Heat waves
glide and twist around you. You walk in the earth's oven.

It is a heat that works inward through the body. You
feel it spiking the marrow of your bones, tightening about
your heart, and sapping every muscle. To lie down in this
heat is to invite death. To keep walking seems only to
delay it.

Now imagine in this corrosive journey a bulge in the
distance, a swelling that defies the illusions all about you
with its solidity. You step toward it as the one thing that
doesn't shift and slide in a land where everything else
does. You expect it to disappear momentarily. But you
begin running to it, and the rock looms ahead of you. It is
firm, intractable, a refuge.

You touch its solid flank and sink into the comforting
arms of its shadow.

Such an imaginary journey is necessary, perhaps, to understand the biblical theme of Jesus as a rock in a weary land. Biblical people were, in a very real sense, far more conscious of land and climate than we are today. They had no technology to create artificial climates in their homes or churches. They lived closer to the land, and the imaginary journey we have taken is close to their reality.

The rock signaled relief, comfort, a place to draw aside and rest. It was a solid structure in a changing world, a place to stand.

But while it was surrounded by waste desert regions, Palestine was also a land of jagged mountain terrain. In times of danger, the people would often retreat to the mountain rocks, for they signified a sure and safe protection. The Benjaminites were nearly destroyed before they took refuge in the rocks of Rimmon (Judg. 20:47). Similarly, when he was persecuted by Saul, David often took refuge in the rocks. Rocks afforded protection and security.

It's little wonder, then, that many modern hymns and popular Christian songs call Jesus the Rock. "Jesus is the rock of our salvation," goes one popular song. "On Christ, the solid rock, I stand; all other ground is sinking sand," proclaims another. One enduring hymn, "Rock of Ages," professes that the rock is "cleft for me" and pleads, "let me hide myself in thee."

In the Bible itself, God is frequently known as the Rock, both in the Old Testament and the New Testament. The name is given to God because he is the strength, the protection, the security of his people. "The Lord is my rock, and my fortress. . . . who is a rock, except our God?" affirms the psalmist (18:2, 31). God is the rock, says Moses in Deuteronomy 32:4, and he adds in verse 31 that this rock is superior to all the symbolic rocks of the surrounding nations.

It is no coincidence that God often chose to reveal

himself in rocky places. In Exodus 17:6, the Lord says, "I will stand before you there on the rock at Horeb." Like a rock, our God is an enduring protector.

2 THESSALONIANS 3:3

But the Lord is faithful; he will strengthen you and guard you from evil.

PRAYER

Too often, Lord, life seems like a desert place.
The heat pounds upon me,
the winds whine,
and I feel lost.
It is then, Lord, that I run to the Rock.
Prepare a place for me, Lord.
Shelter me, protect me, as the
Rock of all ages.

SIX
ROCK:
REDEEMER

The rock represents to the Hebrew nation a strong and glorious protection, a God who is exalted over all gods. But it also becomes associated with sacrifices to this great God. Often rocks served as altars upon which a grateful people laid their thank offerings to the Lord (Josh. 9:30, 31; Judg. 13:19). The sign was always clear: God, the Rock, cares for his people; therefore, on the rock we offer our thanks. Over and over, the Hebrew people are reminded that God brought water out of the rock (Num. 20:8, 11), that God stood before them on the rock (Exod. 17:6), that God endures as the Rock (2 Sam. 22:32).

But increasingly in the Old Testament, the rock becomes allied directly with redemption. In Psalm 19:14, David calls God "my rock and my redeemer." Again in Psalm 89:26, God is called "the Rock of my salvation."

The figure of God the Rock is an amazingly consistent but flexible theme throughout the Old Testament—consistent because of its common reference to the enduring Lord, flexible because of the variety of its uses. Revelation, power, security, redemption—all these qualities characterize our God, the Rock. For someone to be a redeemer, after all, that person first must be revealed, have the power to deliver people from sin, and provide security against future captivity.

But with the prophetic books of the Old Testament, an interesting variation in the image of the rock occurs. In fact, Isaiah claims that the rock will be "a stone of offense . . . to both houses of Israel" (8:14). The will of the Lord has been made clear; redemption has been offered. When people refuse to offer their praise to God in lives of obedience, when they willfully reject his redemption, the very Rock of salvation will be a stumbling stone to them.

This is the key issue: The Rock finally will divide the redeemed from the damned. One cannot have it both ways. If one wants to rest on the Rock, he has to be obedient to the Lord of the universe. If one refuses that blessed rest, the very same Rock will crush him. The passage from Isaiah is recalled by the author of Romans (9:32) and again by Peter, who says bluntly, "they stumble because they disobey the word" (1 Pet. 2:8).

The theme is echoed by the minor prophets. The people of Israel wander in a wasteland, looking for a rock that will provide security, ignoring the safe haven that already has been established from all eternity. These people have made of themselves a rock, a hardness of heart so solid no grace can break through. Having resigned themselves to the wasteland, says the prophet Amos, "They shall wander from sea to sea, and from north to east; they shall run to and fro, to seek the word of the Lord, but they shall not find it" (Amos 8:12).

PSALM 18:1-3
I love thee, O Lord, my strength.
The Lord is my rock, and my fortress,
and my deliverer,
my God, my rock, in whom I take refuge,
my shield, and the horn of my salvation,
my stronghold.

I call upon the Lord, who is worthy to be praised,
and I am saved from my enemies.

PRAYER

When others would lead me
from the Rock,
their paths lead to the desert,
their paths are empty and lonely.
Keep me, Lord, in the shadow of the Rock,
in the presence of my fortress
and my deliverer.

SEVEN
ROCK: CORNERSTONE

In the Old Testament, God promised to establish a rock that would be either a redeemer or a stumbling stone to all nations. In the New Testament, God reveals this rock—Jesus Christ.

The tie between Jesus and the Old Testament image of the rock couldn't be clearer. One of the most meaningful miracles of God occurred when the Hebrew people were wandering in the wilderness after the Exodus from Egypt. The people were suffering the excruciating anguish of thirst—and also a drought of faith. They moaned to Moses, begging for water. Exodus 17:6 recounts how, in his mercy, God responded by bringing water from a rock. "I will stand before you there on the rock at Horeb," said the Lord, and the rock gushed with living water. That miracle always abided in Hebrew memory as a sign of the closeness and power of their God.

In his first letter to the Corinthians, Paul refers specifically to this miracle, but points out that the early Hebrews "drank from the supernatural Rock which followed them, and the Rock was Christ" (1 Cor. 10:4). So in reference to this significant miracle, Jesus, too, is called the Rock. But does the image of the rock mean something different in the New Testament?

Because Jesus and God are one, we would have to say that the rock connotes the same meanings when applied to Jesus as when applied to God. But the rock is also used in a special sense as a name for Jesus. Jesus is the Rock, but he is a unique rock. He is the cornerstone of our faith, the foundation of our belief.

Jesus often used parables in his ministry to make the incomprehensible readily apparent to his followers. He once told the parable of two men who built homes (Matt. 7:24-27). While one man built his house on a sandy foundation which, like the desert, seemed always to slip and slide, another man built his house on a solid rock. When the storms came—all those temptations of Satan that would threaten our faith—the house built on the rock stood firm, while the other house perished. The point of the parable was as plain to Jesus' listeners as it is to us. One needs a sure, unchanging foundation for his faith, and that foundation is Jesus himself.

But perhaps the parable is not quite so simple as it appears to be. We recall that Jesus himself said that "for those outside everything is in parables; so that they may indeed see but not perceive, and may indeed hear but not understand; lest they should turn again, and be forgiven" (Mark 4:11, 12). Jesus was keenly aware that many people would ignore the foundation he offers. While Jesus described himself as the cornerstone (Matt. 21:42), the new rock of faith upon which the whole Christian church would be built, he recognized that many would neglect this cornerstone. Many would choose to build their houses of faith on the sliding sands of the delusive desert.

While Jesus is the cornerstone of all biblical teaching— "You are . . . members of the household of God, built upon the foundation of the apostles and prophets, Christ Jesus himself being the cornerstone" (Eph. 2:19, 20)— many will reject him. A terrible judgment accompanies this rejection. "To you therefore who believe, he is precious, but for those who do not believe, 'The very stone which the builders rejected has become the head of the corner,' and 'A stone that will make men stumble, a rock that will make them fall' " (1 Pet. 2:7, 8).

To all who refuse to accept Jesus as the cornerstone of Christian faith, the cornerstone itself will become a stumbling stone.

2 TIMOTHY 2:19
But God's firm foundation stands,
bearing this seal: "The Lord knows those who are his,"
and, "Let every one who names the name of the Lord
depart from iniquity."

PRAYER
Teach me silence, Lord,
to know you through your words.
Help me to sit still
and to let you help me to understand
your will, your way, your salvation.

EIGHT
ROCK:
LORD

The ministry of Jesus is approaching its climax. Out of his great compassion, Jesus daily performs miracles for the multitudes of people who now follow him. He casts out demons, heals the deformed, restores sight to the blind and speech to the dumb. The multitudes surge around him—the hungry, desperate, and diseased. Jesus' great power radiates into a dark and lonely world. The crowd around him grows so huge—four thousand men, in addition to women and children—that Jesus performs a miracle of multiplying food simply to let them all eat. It seems events press in upon him, that all of time narrows, hardens toward the great battle at Golgotha.

And always, like sharp weapons pointed at him, come the barbs of the Pharisees and Sadducees. His enemies seem never to leave him now. Wherever he goes, their dark, cutting presence is nearby, testing him, demanding signs, pushing relentlessly and cruelly along the path that leads to Golgotha.

Finally Jesus leaves the crowds. How weary he must be by the time he and his disciples encamp near Caesarea Philippi. They discover themselves without food—not even a loaf of bread. After Jesus' miracle of feeding the thousands, this lack must be a bitter irony to the little band of disciples. Here they are, ravaged with hunger, incredibly weary, drained of all strength like an empty lake.

How tiring it must be also to Jesus as he attempts to lift their spirits and redirect their flagging willpower to the even greater needs that lie before them. Is Jesus thinking of the cross at this time?

"Who do men say that the Son of Man is?" he asks the little band (Matt. 16:13). The question is appropriate: Are we doing this for our own sake? Are we merely serving a temporal kingdom? Is it all worth it?

The disciples murmur the answers they have heard. "Some say John the Baptist," says one. Another: "Others say Elijah . . . Jeremiah or one of the prophets" (Matt. 16:14). Yes, all great spiritual leaders. Heroes of the faith. But none of them great enough. All of them great only because they were forerunners of one who is greater than they.

Jesus sharpens the question: "But who do *you* say that I am?"

The outspoken one, Simon Peter, replies, "You are the Christ, the Son of the living God" (Matt. 16:16). What resoluteness in his voice, what assurance. Here before him stands the *One* for whom John the Baptist, Elijah, and Jeremiah were forerunners and prophets—Jesus, the Lord of Lords.

As Jesus blesses Peter for his answer, he says emphatically: "You are Peter, and on this rock I will build my church, and the powers of death shall not prevail against it" (Matt. 16:18). But to what rock is he referring? What rock is sufficient to serve as the cornerstone upon which all believers of all earthly time will build? Peter?

Surely there is a suggestion of this interpretation since Peter's name, Cephas, means "the rock." But this is neither the time nor the place for a mere play on Peter's name. The rock upon which the church will be built is Peter's confession that Jesus is Lord, the very Son of the most high God. This confession provides both the eternal security of which the Old Testament prophets spoke and the great division among peoples they also foretold—a division between those who confess Jesus as Lord and those who deny his godhood and lordship.

It is in relation to this confession that Jesus becomes the head cornerstone—or the stumbling stone. There is no possible way to avoid calling him Lord, for it will be done either in this life or at the eternal judgment when *every* knee shall bow (Phil. 2:10, 11). The lordship of Jesus, our Rock and Redeemer, will not be denied. For those who fail to confess Jesus as Lord in this life, the Rock is the stumbling stone spoken of in Matthew 21:44, Luke 20:18, and Romans 9:33. But for those who accept Christ's lordship, the Rock will be the foundation for their faith, their lives, and their eternities.

JOHN 3:36

He who believes in the Son has eternal life;
he who does not obey the Son shall not see life,
but the wrath of God rests upon him.

PRAYER

Jesus, there is a great divide between man and God,
a chasm between my sin and your perfection.
But you have made a bridge,
and it was made on the cross.
Thank you, Jesus, for being the bridge builder,
for giving me a way back to you.

NINE
LIVING WATER: GIFT OF MERCY

No other known planet has it. Yet earth has it in such abundance that it does more than sustain life. It cleanses. It cools. It heats. Water, like God's grace, is a precious gift. Without it, there can be no physical nor spiritual life. But once bestowed, we receive it in abundance beyond measure.

It is surprising just how often water is described in the Bible. It would be a staggering task simply to list all the references to water in Scripture. Even the major events involving water form a bulky account. From Genesis, where we find the initial portrait of the Spirit moving across the face of the waters, to Revelation, where the saints are invited to wash and drink in the living stream, water has tremendous force and significance.

One of the first acts of Creation involved God's control over water. He separated seas and land masses under the new light so that life could flourish.

That control never relents. At God's direction, the waters collect to inundate the world in the great flood of Noah. On three occasions in the Old Testament, bodies of water part—the Red Sea once and the Jordan River twice—to allow God's people to go forth at his will. At

God's word, water turns to blood and water gushes from a rock.

Through it all, two things become clear. First, God has absolute control over this vital life source, as he does over all things. People do not control it. In our time, men may manipulate water—that is, use it to cool exhaust stacks, supply energy, or heat homes. But this manipulation is of a gift supplied priorly by someone with absolute control.

Second, water throughout the Old Testament clearly becomes associated with God's mercy. God *gives* water because he *loves* his people. That giving and loving typify the nature of God.

But the value of a gift is gauged by one's need for it.

During one period in my life, a relative gave me a new billfold for Christmas for five successive years. Now, I expect a billfold just to get nicely broken in after three years and to last for ten years. By the time I received my fifth billfold, I was gritting my teeth.

God's mercy is a different matter. We can never get enough of it. We thirst for it like water. This desire is emphasized particularly in the prophetic books of the Old Testament.

In Isaiah's time, water was withheld from the land for several years to remind the people of their need for God. The prophetic books become increasingly plaintive. The prophets long for the time when "all the stream beds of Judah shall flow with water" (Joel 3:18). Amos prophesies in the name of the Lord:

"I also withheld the rain from you
when there were yet three months to the harvest;
I would send rain upon one city,
and send no rain upon another city;
one field would be rained upon,
and the field on which it did not rain withered;
so two or three cities wandered to one city to drink water,
and were not satisfied;
yet you did not return to me," says the Lord. (Amos 4:7, 8)

It is as if the Lord, through his power, withholds water and mercy from his people to redirect them to himself— and to the coming One who calls himself the Living Water.

TITUS 3:4-7

*But when the goodness and loving kindness of God
our Savior appeared, he saved us, not because of deeds
done by us in righteousness, but in virtue of his own mercy,
by the washing of regeneration and renewal
    in the Holy Spirit,
which he poured out upon us richly
through Jesus Christ our Savior,
so that we might be justified by his grace
and become heirs in hope of eternal life.*

PRAYER

*Spirit of the Living God, flow fresh on me;
cleanse me,
purify me,
flow through me.
Thank you, Jesus, for living water.*

TEN
LIVING WATER: COMMUNITY HOPE

T. S. Eliot describes a people who have lost all sense of the sacred in his great poem "The Waste Land" (*The Waste Land and Other Poems*, New York: Harcourt, Brace and World, 1934). Their inner spirits are mirrored in the desolate landscape of the desert:

Here is no water but only rock
Rock and no water and the sandy road
The road winding above among the mountains
Which are mountains of rock without water
If there were water we should stop and drink
Amongst the rock one cannot stop or think.

The people in Eliot's spiritual wasteland—and at this point in his personal life, he was one among them—hurry frenzied through the dry places looking for solace. They find no place of rest. Not until his first great Christian poems did Eliot himself identify it.

Who then made strong the foundations and made
fresh the springs
Made cool the dry rock and made firm the sand,

he asks in "Ash Wednesday." In his recognition of God's
control and God's mercy, Eliot discovers "Our peace in His
will."

Life must have resembled a wasteland to those who
were expecting a Messiah as they wandered in a dry
land. They could only remember the life-giving hand of
God who made water gush from the rock.

Palestine, during the time of the late prophets and the
time of Jesus, was surrounded by large stretches of arid
land. A stiff wind from the Mediterranean slapped the
raw, sunburnt face of the land. As the land fell away to
the south, it was stippled by badlands. Wind-blasted rocks
formed weird shapes and cairns, the sides of rocky hills
appearing like thick animal hide worn brittle and crusted
by the heat. The appalling aridity of much of the land
today still bespeaks the pricelessness of water then. Over
seventy ancient sites in Palestine have taken their place
names from the word *ain* meaning spring, and another
sixty use the word *bîr* meaning well. People staked their
lives and futures on these small springs of water. Battles
were fought to retain a single well. Water was more
precious than life, for it was life itself.

Water, then, signified for the Israelites more than a
quenching of thirst, a source of energy, or a means of
bathing. Water signified, first, the presence of life. And
signs of its absence were all around the people: the
blasted clump of weeds, the desiccated tamarisk tree, the
withered fig tree. One wonders how they would have
craved the water that drips from a leaky faucet, how they
would have stood amazed at clouds of steam from an
exhaust stack, how they might have wept before a
polluted stream.

Second, water signified unity. Families and tribes gained
their identity as a community around a common spring or
well.

Third, water represented a hope for the future.
Somehow, with the prospect of water, the future not only

could be endured, but could be filled with promise. The Promised Land of the exiled Israelites was always a land *flowing* with milk and honey.

Life, unity, hope—water represented much more than a liquid substance to the people of Israel.

Life, unity, hope—we can find them today in the One who first put water in the desert.

1 CHRONICLES 28:9

"And you, Solomon my son,
know the God of your father,
and serve him with a whole heart
and with a willing mind;
for the Lord searches all hearts,
and understands every plan and thought.
If you seek him, he will be found by you;
but if you forsake him, he will cast you off for ever."

PRAYER

Lord, as you did with David,
you have placed reminders of your grace all around me—
the pure whiteness of winter snow,
the soft washing of spring rain,
the rustle of rivers and streams.
Let them lead me, Lord,
to serve you with a whole heart
and a willing mind.

ELEVEN
LIVING WATER:
AGENT OF CLEANSING

We have seen, then, that to the Hebrews, water was more
than the chemical formula we objectively label H_2O.
Water signified something for the whole community.
Around wells and springs, communities gathered. They
dared plan a future. They dared hope.

Out of the very life patterns of the people, water came
to represent certain community goals.

But water also represented specific spiritual acts:
cleansing and mercy.

True, water washes away dirt. But the Old Testament
conception of cleansing was more powerful than just a
physical act. Washing is used to represent renewal.

For years I have enjoyed gardening and raising an
array of flowers. I plant the spring beds as early as
September. Before the last splash of gray snow has left,
tulips, hyacinths, and daffodils drill their flashy colors in
the spring yard. When they are on their last, wilting legs,
others begin to break the soil—summer asters, dahlias,
and zinnias. Zinnias are a particularly beautiful summer
flower—a handful of colored sunlight bursting at the end
of a green fuse. Also, they are a hardy flower, blooming
for weeks on end, ever richer and fuller.

But only if they have sufficient water.

One summer I happened to be gone during a particularly dry week early in their growing period. While I was gone, dust choked the young blossoms. When I returned, they looked like staggered soldiers after hard battle.

I hosed them down, thoroughly and heavily. They needed more than water to fill their flaccid veins. They needed cleansing. Already the following morning, the newly washed plants had caught a new vigor. One could almost see them grow and reach for the sun.

Likewise, God's cleansing does more than wash away dirt. It provides spiritual energy, vigor, renewed life.

Often, washing with water in the Bible represents such a purifying, invigorating act. For example, in Exodus 29:4 Aaron and his sons are directed to be washed with water, not to cleanse them of physical dirt, but to signify spiritual purity before the Lord. In the Psalms, washing with water often represents a similar cleansing from sin (Ps. 51:2, 7).

Because it was so scarce in a dry land, water was always highly valued. Water marked ceremonies of worship and friendship. To give water to another person was to give more than just refreshment. It meant bestowing something precious and treasured—a gift of oneself. It was also an act of mercy. To someone in need, the gift of water was extended.

To withhold this gift was a terrible thing. When Job's friends meet with him to find just cause for Job's affliction, Eliphaz suggests that the suffering was brought upon Job because "You have given no water to the weary to drink" (Job 22:7).

In the same way, God withheld water to make the people mindful of their need for him. Because of the Israelites' sin of turning away from God, Isaiah says, "The Lord, the Lord of hosts, is taking away from Jerusalem and from Judah stay and staff, the whole stay of bread, and the whole stay of water" (Isa. 3:1). Instead of mercy, unity, and hope, says Isaiah, the Lord will give them "the water of affliction" (30:20).

As the prophets begin to point to Jesus' coming, the importance of water—and mercy—becomes more poignant. Isaiah captures the theme well. If the people will turn from their evil and seek the Lord, he says, then: "I will pour water on the thirsty land, and streams on the dry ground; I will pour my Spirit upon your descendants, and my blessings on your offspring. They shall spring up like grass amid waters, like willows by flowing streams" (Isa. 44:3, 4).

Only in Jesus, the Living Water, can a thorough cleansing from sin be effected so that the promise of this passage may be fulfilled.

1 JOHN 3:2, 3

Beloved, we are God's children now;
it does not yet appear what we shall be,
but we know that when he appears
we shall be like him,
for we shall see him as he is.
And every one who thus hopes in him
purifies himself as he is pure.

PRAYER

I would be your servant.
I am ready to take the part
You have given me.
Lord, purify my heart
with your Spirit sent
from the well of living water.

TWELVE
LIVING WATER: SOURCE OF LIFE

Jesus came as the fulfillment of Old Testament prophecy, including those that anticipate God's waters of mercy. Jeremiah, for example, describes God as "the fountain of living waters" (Jer. 2:13; 17:13). In the New Testament, Jesus becomes the incarnation of Living Water.

Early in Jesus' ministry, the Pharisees already perceived the threat he posed to their works-oriented religion. The Pharisees proclaimed salvation by the Law; a person always had to do the right things to earn his salvation. Little did they realize that in Jesus all is Yea and Amen (2 Cor. 1:20)—the praise to God—and in him the Law is fulfilled in mercy like streams of water freely poured out. The conflict is made poignantly clear when Jesus, at the Pharisees' urging, is driven out of Judea into Samaria because so many people were being baptized in his name. His was a baptism not into the Law, but into grace, through cleansing from sin.

In Samaria, Jesus comes at length to the small town of Sychar, marked by the place where Jacob had constructed a well. The conjunction of Jacob, the forerunner who built the well, and Jesus, the fulfillment who is the Living Water, is startling. At the well, Jesus asks a Samaritan woman to give him a drink. When she expresses surprise that a Jew would ask a Samaritan for water, Jesus replies: "If you knew the gift of God, and who it is that is saying to you, 'Give me a drink,' you would have asked him and he would have given you living water" (John 4:10). When the woman asks the source of this living water, Jesus says, "Who ever drinks of the water that I shall give him will never thirst; the water that I shall give him will become in him a spring of water welling up to eternal life" (John 4:14).

Jesus comes to us, as to the Samaritan woman, as the Living Water, the very substance of life. He fulfills Old Testament expectations, for in him, there is hope and a future security. One need never thirst again because this water springs up to eternal life. One need never wander in the wasteland of sin again because this water redeems us. Jesus, however, expects certain actions in response to his merciful gift of eternal life.

No one is permitted to simply hoard this water while others perish of thirst. Whoever gives a cup of cold water to drink, says Jesus in Matthew 10:42, shall not lose his reward. Mercy begets mercy. Jesus requires us to extend mercy, to be his image bearers in a world parched for the living waters of his grace.

This two-way mercy—living water received from Jesus and, in turn, given to the world—is an issue of paramount importance to the Christian life. If water is hoarded, dammed up, and blocked off, it simply evaporates or grows stale. In the same way, the Christian life grows dry and sterile if it is not shared. By definition, Christians are vessels through which Christ, the Living Water, flows. In John 7:38, Jesus says: "He who believes in me, as the scripture has said, 'Out of his heart shall flow rivers of living water.' "

The mandate is clear: Christians are channels of Jesus' grace, outpourers of Living Water on the parched spiritual lives of others.

PROVERBS 24:11, 12

Rescue those who are being taken away to death;
hold back those who are stumbling to the slaughter.
If you say, "Behold, we did not know this,"
does not he who weighs the heart perceive it?
Does not he who keeps watch over your soul know it,
and will he not requite man according to his work?

PRAYER

Lord, human need cries out all around me.
There is so much to do
to bring your kingdom into this world.
Yet I withhold the living water.
I fail to reach out to those who are perishing.
I fail to protect those—the elderly,
the unborn, the sick, and the dying—
who are being led to the slaughter.
By your power in me, Lord,
help me to be a channel of your grace
to all of these.

THIRTEEN
LIVING WATER: CHANNEL OF GRACE

As a young boy, I and my friends would often bicycle to a nearby lake to go swimming. The lake was fed by an underground spring, which we couldn't see. Sometimes we would guess where the spring was located. Once a man who had conducted scientific studies of the lake chatted with us and explained with great precision not only where the spring was but how heavily it flowed into the lake.

In a sense, our understanding of that lake parallels our experience as Christians. In our youth, we simply enjoyed the lake, cooling off on a sultry August day in its pure, flowing water. We knew there was a source, but we were content to enjoy its outpouring without knowing its location.

Initially, we receive Jesus' grace like that. We are cleansed and refreshed by bathing in his living water. But we also learn in time the source of this blessing. We grow in our desire to understand the Giver of the Gift, the spring without which there would be no lake.

At the southern end of the lake where I used to swim was a lowland where water collected. Gray trees, their trunks and limbs coated with moss, poked their crooked limbs up from the festering, stagnant swamp. The air, untouched by breezes that washed across the nearby lake, held a stench of decay. It was gloomy and dark. Old trees leaned over and their roots poked up like great fists shaking at us. The dead limbs were bleached white like skeletons. The water was coated with green slime so thick we could spot the trails of water snakes winding through it. Bubbles rose through the scum. If one threw a rock into the water it made a dull, plopping sound like someone choking.

The swamp had once received the same living water that fed the lake. But while the lake was laced with dozens of tiny streams that flowed outward, the bog was a self-contained lowland. Without an outlet, the water had turned deadly stagnant, alive only with the snakes that rippled silently across its surface.

Living water is flowing water. Living water sees a need and offers a cup of cold, fresh water. Those who have living water visit the sick, the poor, the imprisoned. "As you did it to one of the least of these my brethren," Jesus says, "you did it to me" (Matt. 25:40).

During the Jewish Feast of Tabernacles, Jesus went into the temple to teach. He concluded his teaching with these ringing words: "If any one thirst, let him come to me and drink. He who believes in me, as the scripture has said, 'Out of his heart shall flow rivers of living water' " (John 7:37, 38). The two necessarily go together in the Christian life—the inflowing spring of living water from Jesus to us, the outpouring of living water from us to others.

ROMANS 6:6-8
We know that our old self was crucified with him
so that the sinful body might be destroyed,
and we might no longer be enslaved to sin.
For he who has died is freed from sin.

But if we have died with Christ,
we believe that we shall also live with him.

PRAYER

Jesus, when your living water floods my soul,
you become one with me,
and I become one with you.
This is my joy:
That nothing—neither death, nor life,
nor angels, nor principalities,
nor things present, nor things to come,
nor powers, nor height, nor depth,
nor anything else in all creation—
will be able to separate me from the love of God
in Christ Jesus my Lord.

FOURTEEN
LIVING WATER: PROMISE OF ETERNITY

Becoming one with Jesus—so that his will is our will, his love our love, his mercy our mercy—is the hope and challenge of the Christian life.

Most schoolchildren know the chemical formula for water—H_2O, two parts hydrogen to one part oxygen. But in a cup of water, which is which? We have all felt raindrops patter on our skin during a light summer rain. But in the puddle after the rain, where are the individual drops?

In a sense, the sacrament of baptism is just such a merging with Jesus, the Living Water. The word baptism derives from the Greek word *baptizo* meaning "to merge with." In baptism, we die with Christ and are raised with him. This truth is expressed in the sixth chapter of Romans: "Do you not know that all of us who have been baptized into Christ Jesus were baptized into his death? We were buried therefore with him by baptism into death, so that as Christ was raised from the dead by the glory of the Father, we too might walk in newness of life" (Rom. 6:3, 4). Just as blood and water—the redemption and the life—flowed from Jesus' side on the cross, so we, too, die to ourselves in order to be reborn in him.

Our merging with Jesus constitutes the great and glorious vision of the book of Revelation. Just as we experience oneness with Jesus in this life, so one day we will be merged eternally with him in that land of the "river of the water of life, bright as crystal, flowing from the throne of God and of the Lamb" (Rev. 22:1).

Here there will be nothing unclean; here all will be made new. There will be no more night, no more sorrow, when we drink of the river of eternal life. For the Christian, the experience of eternal life begins in this life as he is merged with Christ to share his burden, his glory, and his mission—bringing Living Water to the thirsty.

So when the prophet Isaiah calls, "Ho every one who thirsts, come to the waters" (Isa. 55:1), he foresees a time when God "will swallow up death for ever, and the Lord God will wipe away tears from all faces" (Isa. 25:8). In this life, we still have to contend with our tears. Our quest to do the will of Jesus is often met with sorrow and frustration. We are imperfect vessels in an imperfect world.

But in that new world, which is watered by the crystal stream, every tear shall be wiped away. Those who have sought to follow the Savior will find tears banished. We will be able to answer unfalteringly to our Lord's invitation: "The Spirit and the Bride say, 'Come.' And let him who hears say, 'Come.' And let him who is thirsty come, let him who desires take the water of life without price" (Rev. 22:17, 18).

What a joy, however, that we who thirst can also drink of that Living Water now, letting it flow fresh and clean through us in this life.

ISAIAH 35:6, 7
For waters shall break forth in the wilderness,
and streams in the desert;

the burning sand shall become a pool,
and the thirsty ground springs of water.

PRAYER
Lord, you alone can bring life,
you alone can make the desert blossom,
you alone can create springs in a dry land.
I pray for this living water,
by which all is made fresh and new.

FIFTEEN
GOOD SHEPHERD: DEFENDER

Shepherding was one of the earliest occupations of ancient peoples, including the Israelites, who already had sizable herds when they departed Mesopotamia for Canaan. Moreover, shepherding was always considered an honorable profession; there was nothing second class about it. King David, God's anointed and Israel's best-loved king, was a shepherd. Amos, the prophet from Tekoa, was a shepherd, and his prophetic writings were enriched by liberal allusions to the flock of his people Israel. Many Old Testament writers similarly referred to the people of Israel as a flock of sheep.

The references had several clear implications. Philip Keller says in his book *A Shepherd Looks at Psalm 23* (Grand Rapids, Mich.: Zondervan, 1970):

It is no accident that God has chosen to call us his sheep. The behavior of sheep and human beings is similar in many ways. . . . Our mass mind (or mob instincts), our fears and timidity, our stubbornness and stupidity, our perverse habits are all parallels of profound importance.

Sheep were animals that often strayed from their flock. Particularly in the rugged hills of Palestine, where the vegetation was sparse, sheep might be inclined to wander in search of food into dangerous, rocky areas infested by snakes and animals of prey.

Yet sheep were a valuable resource to the people of Israel. They provided not only a simple source of food or wool for clothing, but also an important type of sacrifice. As a result, they were carefully protected. A shepherd's role was crucial.

Good shepherds knew their flocks well, and their flocks knew the shepherd. One of the most revealing works about the nature of a good shepherd is the Twenty-third Psalm of the Shepherd-King David, a psalm richly elaborated in the book by Philip Keller mentioned above. In a direct comparison between God and the shepherd, David praises the shepherd's care for his flock. The shepherd leads his sheep to green pastures and quiet waters, restores them, protects them from evil, and watches over them.

With the high regard for the profession of shepherding in the Hebrew nation, it is little wonder that the prophets spoke of the Lord as a Shepherd who would gather his wandering people (Isa. 40:10, Jer. 31:10). And when Jesus specifically declared *he* was the Good Shepherd (John 10:14), he did so as the fulfillment of these prophetic expectations. Again we see not some strange and foreign title for Jesus, but a simple name so engrained in the life of the people as to be held more precious.

But today many of us have never even seen sheep. Can the title of shepherd have any significance for us? Can Jesus still be *our* shepherd? Perhaps we can best answer these questions by looking at the ways Jesus continues to shepherd us. For instance, he protects us against danger.

It is almost startling to picture a shepherd as a warrior and defender. We tend to associate the shepherding profession with great gentleness, and to a certain extent, this is true. The shepherd is gentle with his flock, but because he loves them, he will also defend them from any threat. The hills of Palestine were a preying ground for many beasts. Snakes, including deadly vipers, slid among the rocks. Lions lurked under cover. Hyenas roved in vicious packs. Even bears would come down from forested regions. The shepherd's defenses—a staff and sling—seem to us so frail. Yet he was a man of great courage and, if necessary, would engage in hand-to-hand combat to guard his flock.

What an assurance to know that the Lord continues to shepherd us. Jesus has not left us defenseless. When we read a passage such as Romans 8:35-39 with its assertion that nothing—not even demons nor powers—can separate us from the love of Jesus, we know that our Good Shepherd remains beside us our warrior and defender.

1 JOHN 3:1
See what love the Father has given us,
that we should be called children of God.

PRAYER
When I wander into dangerous places, Lord,
places where I am afraid or lonely,
shepherd me;
prepare a place for me;
lead me to gentle waters.

SIXTEEN
GOOD SHEPHERD: PROVIDER OF REST

Jesus speaks of himself not only as the Good Shepherd, but also as the door of the sheepfold, an entrance to perfect rest and security where we "shall be saved, and will go in and out and find pasture" (John 10:9).

We are struck by how many people expend the brief span of their lives in a frantic search for peace. The more desperately they seek, the more elusive peace seems. Henry David Thoreau was right, perhaps, when he said in his book *Walden*, published in 1854, "Why should they begin digging their graves as soon as they are born?" He adds that man "has no time to be anything but a machine." We seek and seek and seem to lose sight of a goal in the very act of seeking.

And in the frenetic pace of modern life, we often try to fill that goal by vacations.

My family has grown to love camping. I don't recommend it for everyone, but it is a wonderful vacation for us. A curious thing happens when we camp. Let me illustrate.

When we leave the house in our overpacked car, our list of preparations is carefully checked off—we have packed the silverware, taken the dog to a keeper, replaced the broken tent stakes, and purchased fresh batteries for the flashlight. In addition, I always have my own private list to check off. I pack books, a newspaper, and a stack of magazines I have been wanting to read but haven't yet found time for.

The first evening at the campsite, I set out with good intentions. Dinner is on time. The campfire starts nicely at dusk. I will be able to complete much of my reading, I think.

But a curious thing happens. Later in the evening, I begin to look into the flickering flames of the campfire instead of the magazine lying open on my lap. I don't *have* to read this article *now,* I think. Instead, one of my children, spotting the drooping magazine, climbs into my lap. The magazine slips out of my hand. (It will be used later to start a campfire.) We hear an owl hoot and listen for it again. We notice stars winking through the pines. In the distance we hear the waves of the lake murmuring a quiet melody we hadn't even noticed before. Where had it been? Or, more accurately, where had we been?

God had spread the evening out for us to read with our hearts. He had provided a quiet place—a shelter almost, it seems—before we arrived there. His Spirit was with us at that place.

The Good Shepherd has prepared a quiet place for each of us. If we come at his invitation, the place is ready. The Old Testament shepherd knew in advance where the shady pastures were, where the quiet waters rippled. He may have led his flock through an arid land, or through valleys of danger and the shadow of death where he protected them. But also he led them to the quiet place of rest. No shepherd would simply wander aimlessly, allowing his sheep to die of thirst or hunger, while he looked around for a green pasture. Nor will our Good Shepherd.

And just as our Good Shepherd provides us with rest and quiet in this life, he also provides us a home of final rest in heaven with him. Jesus has *gone ahead* to prepare a place for us (John 14:2). When at last we enter our eternal rest, he will be waiting for us, arms spread wide to welcome us to his fold.

JOHN 14:27
Peace I leave with you; my peace I give to you;
not as the world gives do I give to you.
Let not your hearts be troubled,
neither let them be afraid.

PRAYER
Into your perfect rest—
a place prepared by you
and by your perfect sacrifice,
a place of perfect
and eternal peace—
I am called, and I answer:
Lord Jesus, come quickly.

SEVENTEEN
GOOD SHEPHERD: SEEKER OF LOST SHEEP

My father never took piano lessons; he played by ear. Now, perhaps, his fingers no longer do what his ear tells them to do, but I can remember as a very young boy sitting in the living room while he played one of his favorite songs, "God Leads Us Along." He played so that I heard the waters ripple in the notes, the fire scorch, and the dangers threaten—so that the victorious chorus rang out: God leads his dear children along! The words of the song are etched in my memory as if I heard them only yesterday.

In shady green pastures,
so rich and so sweet,
God leads His dear children along:
Where the water's cool flow
bathes the weary one's feet,
God leads His dear children along:

Some through the waters, some through the flood,
Some through the fire, but all through the blood;
Some through great sorrow, but God gives a song,
In the night season and all the day long.

Surely Jesus is our guide and our Good Shepherd, as long as we choose to follow him.

Too often, however, we choose our own way.

In the last chapter, I recalled a camping vacation in which I had sensed that God had prepared the place for me before I arrived there. In contrast to that vacation is a trip I took some five years ago. It was planned as a vacation; now I simply call it a trip.

It couldn't have started more perfectly. The translucent blue sky seemed to rise forever into space. A ring of clouds was strung like a necklace where the sky touched down to tree-lined hills. The forests we passed reminded us of past camping vacations. My son recalled the time we had found a fallen oak and tried to count the age rings in its trunk. The count had topped a hundred. And at first, this day seemed to contain the same surprising grandeur, declaring in full song the handiwork that had shaped it.

But things passed too quickly. We rode long and rapidly down I-96 toward Chicago in the old Chevy we had nicknamed the Incredible Hulk. Between the booming bodies of trucks, we caught glimpses of golden sand dunes and a snatch of blue water that had to be Lake Michigan. But as we approached the city, we began to realize this vacation would be unlike others we had taken—vacations squeezed out of empty pockets and patched tents, a Coleman stove and a K-Mart cooler, old sleeping bags that smelled musty from morning dew. This time our camping ground would be a large inn on the north side of Chicago. The trip, we had figured, would let me work at a well-known library nearby and relax with the family on my off-time.

But the off-time was always off. From the motel pool, we counted twelve jets overhead in ten minutes, each belching landing gear and smoke and noise at us as they leveled into O'Hare Airport. Muzak from the loudspeakers by the pool curdled the air like rancid milk. Tired travelers glowered at our small, noisy crew. We found ourselves longing to see the flash of a deer in a deep forest or a fallen oak to count rings on.

We had chosen to go a different way, a way that seemed to appeal to us for rather selfish reasons. Can Jesus be Lord even of vacations? I think so. Not that it is wrong to vacation at inns—nor better to vacation in tents. But this time, we had planned our vacation for ourselves, and even vacations can be planned for God.

Like sheep we had gone astray, pursuing our own way, and the Good Shepherd had needed to seek us out. The Good Shepherd knows each of his sheep by name, and he calls to those who wander. Rather than fearing his voice, it should give us comfort. The Good Shepherd will find us.

PSALM 139:14-16

Thou knowest me right well;
my frame was not hidden from thee,
when I was being made in secret,
intricately wrought in the depths of the earth.
Thy eyes beheld my unformed substance;
in thy book were written, every one of them,
the days that were formed for me,
when as yet there was none of them.

PRAYER

Lord, I want to praise you for all your works and ways,
for your infinite power and wisdom.
I thank you that you know all things;
that you knew me even before I was made,
and that in knowing me
—even with my weakness and faults—
you love me and call me
your child.

EIGHTEEN
GOOD SHEPHERD: DOOR

In the tenth chapter of the Gospel of John, Jesus refers to himself several times as the Good Shepherd. Each time he applies the comparison in a practical way. For example, he is the "door of the sheep" (John 10:7); that is, we only enter rest through Jesus. False shepherds hover all about the gate in an effort to delude us and lead us astray. *Only Jesus* is the door, and Jesus is the *only door.* He alone lays down his life for his sheep. He has paid the supreme price for the cost of admission to his rest.

In addition, Jesus says, "I know my own, and my own know me" (John 10:14). No strays will be permitted to enter the fold nor will anyone, including false shepherds, be able to sneak in. The rest within Jesus' fold is perfect. In ancient Palestine, a shepherd would practice a unique call so if his sheep milled with other flocks, his call would separate his flock from the others. Jesus has called his sheep, and they answer to his voice. No one, he says, can snatch them out of his hand (John 10:28).

But beyond this, Jesus promises to find the straying sheep. He will go into danger to draw the lost and lonely to safety. In one of his best-loved parables, Jesus affirms that even with ninety-nine sheep safely in the fold, the Good Shepherd will not rest until that last, lost one is found (Matt. 18:10-14). Each sheep is precious in Jesus' sight. He knows each one by name. And he wants each one to know him.

In a corner of our house, we have a pump sewing machine inherited years ago from grandmother. Its six drawers are tucked full of aged lace yellowing like rose petals around the edges, of needles and pins we refuse to use. One drawer has six pairs of sunglasses, all the same size, shape, and color. Occasionally we open a drawer, finger the still-shining tools, locate the three pennies in the corner, and close it again. For grandmother, the sewing machine was a kind of hideaway, and we try to keep it that way. Fragments of her personality linger there, fluttering through the rose petal lace, darting through the needles.

That sewing machine corner is a special place in our house. There are many such places or events in our lives—places made special because of treasured communion between human spirits. They are places steeped in quiet where voices speak from long distances, like friends groping for words after long absence; where memories rise and sort through each other and steer their freighted ore toward new directions after having traveled uneven paths; where old doors open, and a fresh wind comes to scatter a new life.

All the places of our lives can become special when we share them with the Good Shepherd. He is the door to abundant life. His Spirit communes with us and enriches even the darkest moments. When we seem to be most lost, the Good Shepherd is seeking us and pointing the way to a rich pasture with quiet waters and overflowing mercy.

We have all, like sheep, gone astray, says the prophet Isaiah (Isa. 53:6). Yet there is One who is willing to hunt down those winding paths of our lives, and in his mercy, lead us to the quiet place he has prepared for us. The Good Shepherd still calls us to come and enjoy his rest.

PHILIPPIANS 4:5-7

The Lord is at hand.
Have no anxiety about anything,
but in everything by prayer and supplication
with thanksgiving let your requests be made
known to God.
And the peace of God,
which passes all understanding,
will keep your hearts and your minds
in Christ Jesus.

PRAYER

As Paul wrote to the Philippians,
encouraging them to "Rejoice in the Lord always;
again I will say, Rejoice,"
so I, too, rejoice in a Savior
who multiplies peace times peace.
May this peace, which passes all understanding,
so dwell in my heart
that anxiety, worry, and care
all pass away.

NINETEEN
GREAT PHYSICIAN: HEALER OF SICKNESS

The Healer, or Physician, is one of the most intriguing names of Jesus because, like the Good Shepherd, it is a name he gives himself. To the scribes and Pharisees, who judged him because he mingled with sinners, Jesus responds, "Those who are well have no need of a physician, but those who are sick. . . . I come not to call the righteous, but sinners" (Matt. 9:12, 13). Like the other names of Jesus, this one places him squarely in the life of the community and emphasizes his solid appropriation of the common, the hurt, and the suffering as his people.

Medical practices of ancient peoples strike us as very rude, even primitive. No sterile operating rooms, precision instruments, or advanced technology existed there. Yet the desire to relieve human pain was no less acute. Since the fall of Adam, man has struggled with how to alleviate the dreadful suffering that accompanies fallen nature.

In biblical times, rampant disease was very much in evidence. Plagues of epidemic proportion were not uncommon. But organic diseases were perhaps even more widespread. Leprosy is a case in point. In addition to true leprosy, known today as Hansen's Disease, the term was used to cover a host of ailments we rarely see today, including boils and fungus infections. Also common were many diseases now routinely treated and cured in the Western world by medical technology—congenital diseases, influenza and pneumonia, and diseases caused by the lack of proper hygiene.

In Jesus' time, treatment for disease was primitive, although less superstitious perhaps in Israel than in surrounding pagan nations. Some treatments are detailed in Scripture—a poultice of figs for boils (Isa. 38:21), wine and oil for wounds (Luke 10:34). Although some of the primitive treatments were effective in healing or alleviating pain, the overall portrait is one of terrible suffering and debilitating pain from sicknesses of many kinds.

Jesus addressed himself to these purely physical infirmities, not simply to alleviate the pain but to drive through the pain to the source of the infirmity itself. His miracles of healing were numerous, and they teach us two important things about our Savior.

First, he cares about our human struggles. He desires our freedom from suffering, and he acts directly against pain. His arm is not shortened, and it extends toward us in mercy to heal.

Second, Jesus hates sickness for he recognizes its source is in sin. Why else would he have fought it so steadfastly in miracle after miracle? Frequently, his miracles of healing were accompanied or activated by an adjuration against sin.

In *Jesus as They Saw Him,* William Barclay puts the image of Jesus the Physician into poignant relief:

The fact that Jesus took to himself the title of physician is the sure sign that he never turns in loathing and repulsion from the sinner, never regards the sinner with disgusted and nauseated contempt, never looks on the sinner as someone to be annihilated and obliterated, but always looks on the sinner as a sufferer needing above all things the healing power of grace.

Jesus' love made him a healer not only of sickness, but also of sin.

JAMES 5:16

Therefore confess your sins to one another,
and pray for one another,
that you may be healed.
The prayer of a righteous man has great power in its effects.

PRAYER

Lord, many today suffer from an illness of body or mind
that seems to lie beyond the help of medicine.
You have said in John 14 that whatever I ask
in your name
you will do it so that the Father may be glorified
in the Son.
In your name, Jesus, I pray for healing.

TWENTY
GREAT PHYSICIAN: HEALER OF SIN

The work of the physician, often allied with the priestly office in the Hebrew tradition, was highly respected in ancient Israel. But there were severe impediments against the acquisition of any practical medical knowledge. The injunctions against uncleanness, for example, helped promote hygiene, but seriously subverted both human compassion and medical expertise. Since a dead body was considered unclean, corpses were usually removed with dispatch—a measure that discouraged the spread of disease but also prevented physicians from doing any autopsies. As a result, doctors were virtually ignorant of human physiognomy.

The Jews also held an incomplete view of the causes of sickness. Most often, they considered disease a result of sin, as indeed it is in general terms of the fall of man. But they often failed to differentiate between the fallen condition of human nature and an individual's sin. To say that anyone who is ill has committed a sin that resulted in his sickness is a grave theological error to which the Hebrew nation was particularly prone. Jesus cut through this theological confusion with his clear love for the sinner *despite* the sin.

Jesus' love did not obscure his recognition that sin first brought suffering into the world. Repeatedly, he drove to the root of man's condition in his miracles of healing. A modern doctor who only treats symptoms is an inadequate doctor. All of his medical training has been designed to help him diagnose the *etiology*, the source of the illness. In the same way, our Great Physician identified the very source of human sickness.

But Jesus does not leave us in our original condition. He has not just the skill, but the *power*—the absolute *authority*—to heal our illness. That is why, over and over in his miracles, Jesus says to those whom he has healed, "Your faith has made you well" (Luke 9:48), or, "Your sins are forgiven" (Luke 5:20). Only in that two-fold act—faith in Jesus' authority and acceptance of his forgiveness of sin—can there be genuine healing.

In Scripture, we sometimes see a pattern wherein God gives up to their sins persons who willfully persist in their wickedness. But the Divine Physician can use even that process to cure the sinner. As the prophet Hosea says, "Come, let us return to the Lord; for he has torn, that he may heal us; he has stricken and he will bind us up" (Hos. 6:1). Then, with direct prophetic reference to Jesus' redemption on the cross, Hosea adds, "After two days he will revive us; on the third day he will raise us up, that we may live before him" (Hos. 6:2).

Herein lies Jesus' perfect healing. He has defeated the last enemy, death: "He will swallow up death forever," says Isaiah (Isa. 25:8). Through Jesus, not only can we be healed of our infirmities, but we can be completely cured of sin and its eternal consequences.

Like any good doctor, Jesus sees us as we are. We are stripped spiritually naked before him. He knows us perfectly, and we can hide nothing from him. But here is a physician who is willing to give his own life so that our disease may be cured.

Modern man has, to a large extent, placed his faith in

the healing powers of science. Some, in fact, claim that
any of Jesus' miracles of healing can be duplicated in any
hospital.

This is simply false. While we surely can thank God for
medical knowledge, since all good gifts come from him,
this knowledge is qualitatively different from that of
Jesus. Jesus has power over sickness. Miracles beggar our
imagination simply because they do not depend upon
intermediary devices. They depend only on Jesus' will.

But the greater miracle is this: If Jesus is truly God, if
he not only died but still lives, if our faith unites us with
him, and his will still prevails, if he is still—as risen Lord
and victor over death—all-powerful, then his healing
power is not diminished and his miracle-working power
can reach into our lives.

1 PETER 2:24

He himself bore our sins in his body on the tree,
that we might die to sin and live to righteousness.
By his wounds you have been healed.

PRAYER

Lord, your all-powerful arm is not shortened,
and I pray that you will reach to me
with your healing power
to make me whole in body and soul.

TWENTY-ONE
RABBI:
TEACHER

Certain teachers have so distinguished themselves in our
experience that in memory they seem to stand before us
even now. Such teachers—whether we recollect them
from first grade, junior high, college, or graduate school—
are remembered not best for what they taught, but for
who they were. We remember what they stood for and
what they stood against, what made them—and us—
laugh, what made them—and us—want to weep. Because
they were living persons with beliefs and emotions, they
touched our lives, and many of us were transformed as a
result.

Teaching is a noble profession, although one much
maligned in our time. There are brilliant people, gifted
with grace and wisdom, in its ranks—and also those who
never should have considered it. Somehow we survive the
latter and rejoice in the former. We wish all of our
teachers were perfect, but they, like us, are afflicted with
human weaknesses.

The wish for a perfect teacher was also common in
Jesus' time.

By then, teaching had been transformed from the
profession as it was known in the ancient world. Just four

hundred years before Christ, the great Greek teachers—
Socrates, Plato, and Aristotle—had attracted students
who sought them out to discuss issues. But increasingly,
schools were established as convenient places for students
and teachers to gather. Curricula were established.
Programs were formed. The wandering teacher—the
one to whom others went for wisdom, advice, and
instruction—all but disappeared. When John the Baptist, a
prophet who was also a kind of teacher, appeared as the
forerunner of the Messiah, he was a voice crying in the
wilderness (Matt. 3:1). The teacher of wisdom was now
an outcast.

The Hebrew nation had also institutionalized education.
Society had become increasingly formal, and religious
orders had usurped the task of teaching. At the time of
Jesus, scribes, Pharisees, and Sadducees used the
synagogue as a forum for education. But to a large
degree, it was an education that had allowed all life to
leak out and be replaced by an ironclad system of facts,
rules, and regulations.

In the nineteenth century, the great novelist Charles
Dickens wrote several books that focused upon education,
the most famous of which is *Hard Times*. For the students
in that book, education was indeed a hard time. The
novel presents a devastating look at education—an
education built on facts alone, an education in which the
surgery of data had ripped out the spirit of man.
Dickens says of one of the regimented characters, a
Mr. Harthouse: "He was touched in the cavity where
his heart should have been—in that nest of addled eggs,
where the birds of heaven would have lived if they had
not been whistled away." The tragedy of an education
built solely on facts and rules is that it leaves little room
for the heart—for belief and wonder—without which life
is an arid wasteland of objective data. Without belief and
without wonder, people become mere things, numbers,
ciphers.

Such was the danger of teaching in Jesus' time also. Law was uppermost, the heart irrelevant. In this context, we begin to understand how radical Jesus' teachings were, for they redirected learning to the great mystery of human belief.

PROVERBS 9:10

The fear of the Lord is the beginning of wisdom,
and the knowledge of the Holy One is insight.

PRAYER

Lord, I pray you
to open my heart to your will,
to renew my wonder before your glory,
to be taught and led by your Spirit.

TWENTY-TWO
RABBI:
AUTHORITY

Charles Dickens has not been alone in his fear of an education solely oriented to facts. In the twentieth century, he was joined by the clear voice of C. S. Lewis. In *The Chronicles of Narnia,* for example, Lewis's children are symbolically captive in a house of learning in which the bars are formed by rigid systems. The children yearn for a fuller, richer, and more meaningful life.

Lewis also wrote a book, *The Abolition of Man* (New York: Macmillan, 1947), that carefully debunks the objective method of modern education. In it, he says the exchange of belief for facts is a bad bargain:

It is the magician's bargain: Give up our soul, get power in return. But once our souls, that is, our selves, have been given up, the power thus conferred will not belong to us. We shall in fact be the slaves and puppets of that to which we have given our souls.

The very title of Lewis's book—*The Abolition of Man*—indicates what has been lost in such learning.

The educational scene depicted by Dickens and Lewis is not unlike that of Jesus' time. The synagogue had developed into a compulsory education system. The children were taught by scribes, and their basic textbook was the Law, or Torah. While Hebrew law, rooted as it was in the divine law given to Moses, was a thoroughly admirable thing, it contained the same danger as any modern law system. Laws degenerated to mere rules. People saw the Law as an end in itself.

In the hands of the scribes, with the backing of the powerful Pharisees, the Law became an increasingly rigid system. A compendium grew around Moses' Law that purported to prescribe God's will in any particular circumstance. The scribes believed there were 613 commandments in the Mosaic Law, 248 of which were positive and 365 negative. But they supplemented even these to cover new situations and the list grew; and as it grew, the people grew further from God. The Law itself became important and all-consuming. Forgotten was the giver of the Law.

For example, in Eden God established the seventh day as a day of rest. When God gave the Law to Moses, he declared that no work should be done on the Sabbath. But the scribes soon specified thirty-nine kinds of work not to be done on the Sabbath, and their list grew with each new circumstance. The clear will of God was lost in details.

Such, then, were the primary teachings of Jesus' day.

But a few teachers seemed to cut through this rigid system of knowledge to wisdom itself. They were called rabbis. The term *rab* meant simply great or master. The rabbi, or master teacher, was learned in the law, but still saw through the Law to its source—God. Since the rabbi was not employed at the synagogue, he owed no special allegiance to any particular *system* of Law. He was free to speak the truth.

Jesus is often called Rabbi, which signifies, first of all, his complete knowledge of the Law. We remember that even as a young boy of approximately twelve, his teaching was so powerful that it astonished the scribes and Pharisees. But he also taught as *one having authority*—and with good reason. Jesus knew the divine lawgiver as no scribe possibly could.

JOHN 8:31, 32

If you continue in my word,
you are truly my disciples,
and you will know the truth,
and the truth will make you free.

PRAYER

To hear amid the noise of this world
the one still, clear Voice
that speaks words of truth
because that Voice is truth itself;
this is my desire,
and in the words of that Voice,
I am free indeed.

TWENTY-THREE
RABBI:
MASTER

Jesus is called Rabbi not only by his own disciples (John 1:38, 49), but also by others, including at least one Pharisee (John 3:2). In a sense, Jesus' reputation is what makes him so dangerous to the established order of his time. His authority and wisdom as a teacher are recognized, but he serves no cause other than God's.

However, Jesus is called not only Rabbi, but also Rabboni, an even more respectful term meaning "my Lord and Master." We find the term used in John 20:16 by Mary Magdalene as she addresses the risen Christ. Rabboni is a term of worship. Jesus, who is the great teacher, is also the Lord of all.

We sometimes may think how sweet it must have been to sit at the feet of this teacher—and students then did sit at their teacher's feet—and listen to his teachings. But Jesus' words live on, both through Scripture and through his presence with us in his Holy Spirit. Our Rabboni lives today.

The huge difference between Jesus and the scribes of his day is that his teachings do not depend on the commentaries for their authority. Jesus himself is the source of all wisdom. In his book *By What Authority*

(Suffolk: Darton, Longman and Todd, 1974), William Barclay comments:

This authority of Jesus was personal, for the thing which amazed his opponents was that, on their standards, he was an uneducated man. "The Jews marvelled at it, saying, How is it that this man has learning, when he has never studied?" (John 7:15). And yet in spite of the fact that he had no technical theological education, his teaching was such that it struck the note of complete authority. Jesus was never afraid to use the word "I". . . . No scribe ever made a statement on his own responsibility; he always quoted this, that, and the next rabbi. If Jesus quoted at all, he quoted scripture; but when he spoke, he spoke on his own authority or, to be more accurate, with the authority of God.

How does one begin to summarize the teachings of the Master Teacher, he whose authority is complete and self-inherent?

Remember once again the acute emphasis placed upon the Law by the teachers of Jesus' day. When Jesus summarizes the Law in his one great commandment, it seems utterly simple and straightforward. He slices through all the intricacies of the commentaries by saying: "This is my commandment, that you love one another as I have loved you" (John 15:12). In a sense, this is Jesus' greatest teaching: Because we have his love, we love others—and ourselves—as he does.

We have remarked, however, that the greatest teachers instruct not so much by facts as by their examples, their actions, their beliefs. As the beloved teacher, the Rabboni, Jesus gives us the primary example for Christian living. Jesus says in John 15:13, "Greater love has no man than this, that a man lay down his life for his friends." But more than just saying the words, Jesus lives them. He lays down his life daily in bearing the burdens of others. He

walks to tiny villages to heal the sick and suffering. He
shares his food. He takes time to console others, to
comfort, to cheer them up. And above all these gifts, he
walks the road no one can share with him to the rugged
crest of Golgotha where he does, in fact, lay down his life
for those he loves, those who love him, and those whom
nobody seems to love. All these are his friends.

Is that the end of it? No, for Jesus continues to share
his love. "I will not leave you desolate," he said (John
14:18). That great source of eternal love which has its
wellspring in our Savior flows to us and through us by
the Holy Spirit.

Jesus' teaching provides us with a *way of living*. The
supreme commandment to love one another does not
replace the Old Testament commandments or make them
meaningless. Rather, it gives them absolute meaning. Jesus
came to fulfill the Law, to show us a higher way. Each
Old Testament law has its New Testament counterpart. By
following the commandments in love, rather than through
an onerous sense of dogged duty, we turn each "thou
shalt not" commandment into a positive "thou shalt."

Jesus' love gives us a sense of majestic self-worth
through which we may lovingly fulfill the Law. "No
longer," says Jesus, "do I call you servants . . . I have
called you friends" (John 15:15). We are not slaves to the
Law. Rather, through Jesus' love, we become his friends.
We are free to be pupils of the Rabboni, the beloved
Master.

2 CORINTHIANS 13:11
Finally, brethren, farewell.
Mend your ways,
heed my appeal,
agree with one another,
live in peace,

and the God of love and peace
will be with you.

PRAYER

O Lord and Master,
may your love fall fresh on me this day
so that I may live your teaching
and lighten the load of someone you love.

TWENTY-FOUR
BRIGHT MORNING STAR

Sometimes modern life seems like a parade in which no one knows the proper route, the starting point, or the final destination. Noise and blare and hurried shouts send loud directions into the air, but we seem to go nowhere.

"Life is a rat race," or "Life is a treadmill," people say. Yet they hurry to join in, afraid of being left behind. Strangely, no one appears to care where the rush leads.

Once I stepped into an elevator that didn't work properly. I felt the sudden rush of motion as we propelled upward, picking up speed. The floor indicators winked out little green numbers as we whirled to a high floor, stopped, then slowly drifted downward. There were other people packed into the tiny, box-like space, but like all elevator crowds, they stared blankly at the door or the winking lights and no one spoke. We were strangers forced into a communion of fear. When the elevator doors finally opened, we were back on the first floor. Some people sighed and stepped off. Others tried again.

Like my unsuccessful elevator ride, we often move through time without reaching any destination. In all the hurry, we wonder if there is any still point. In his famous poem "Choruses from 'The Rock,'" which describes spiritual life in the twentieth century, T. S. Eliot wrote:

Endless invention, endless experiment,
Brings knowledge of motion, but not of stillness;
Knowledge of speech, but not of silence;
Knowledge of words, and ignorance of the Word.
All our knowledge brings us nearer to our ignorance,
All our ignorance brings us nearer to death,
But nearness to death no nearer to God.
Where is the Life we have lost in living?
Where is the wisdom we have lost in knowledge?
Where is the knowledge we have lost in information?
The cycles of Heaven in twenty centuries
Bring us farther from God and nearer to the Dust.

What a vivid example of our restless hurry.

A different picture comes to mind. It is night, past bedtime, and I have walked with my children to the park across the street to watch the stars. As we stand on the blue lawn and look upward at the spangled sky, my youngest child whispers, "They never change—do they, Daddy?"

The stars have been there since God called them into being and flung them across the abyss of all space. We know they do change. They are huge flares of energy that are always shifting and erupting. And yet to us they are unchanging—still and silent and shining in the night sky until Jesus makes the new heaven and the new earth. So sure are they that mariners marked their course by them. So certain are they that we mark our time and our calendars by their fixed motions. The nearest star, the sun, consistently awakens us in the morning and lays us down to sleep at night. Stars are huge and glorious beyond our imagination, yet so familiar in their regularity that we can point to one spot and say, "There, that is the North Star. So it always has been, is, and will be."

And so I said to my children that night as we traced the long curve of the Big Dipper to the North Star. And I thought, it is the same as when my father took me out past bedtime and moved his finger through the dark folds of night toward that radiant beacon of surety.

When we think of all the names and titles given to Jesus, surely one of the most glorious must be the Bright Morning Star (Rev. 22:16). Jesus is our surety in a world of change, a fixed and enduring hope for ages to come.

JOHN 8:12

Again Jesus spoke to them, saying,
"I am the light of the world;
he who follows me will not walk in darkness,
but will have the light of life."

PRAYER

Day by day the heavens utter speech,
declaring in full voice your handiwork,
declaring in full song the symphony
you are.

TWENTY-FIVE
LIGHT OF THE WORLD

In the book of Numbers, the prophet Balaam foretells that "a star shall come forth out of Jacob" (Num. 24:17). That star would be Jesus, the Bright Morning Star described in Revelation. But why was the star used as a name and image for Jesus?

This most beautiful name is rich with significance, for it signals the end of our human darkness. The morning star is *bright;* its splendid glow shatters the night. As John said of Jesus, "The darkness has not overcome it" (John 1:5). Nor can it ever. Moreover, this bright star announces the *morning;* the day of God's kingdom of light is upon us. The announcement goes out to all who see the star.

For similar reasons, Jesus is named the Light (John 1:4, 5, 9). The opening chapter of the Gospel of John may be described as a rhapsody to light. It first describes the glorious and majestic divinity of Jesus; he dwells eternally with the Father and the Holy Spirit. It moves next to the last of the prophets, John the Baptist, who came to bear witness to the light. Third, it moves to the Light of the World, incarnated in Jesus.

Light has always had religious significance, from the ancient Egyptian Pharaohs who proclaimed themselves

sons of the god of light to the druids and the Incas. But
there is only one God of Light—Jesus. And he claims this
name for himself: "I am the light of the world; he who
follows me will not walk in darkness, but will have the
light of life" (John 8:12).

Here is the Light awaited by the prophets, among them
Isaiah. He saw his people enmeshed in terrible darkness,
using wizards, mediums, and the occult to try to break
through it. But these only thickened the darkness: "They
will look to the earth, but behold, distress and darkness,
the gloom of anguish; and they will be thrust into thick
darkness" (Isa. 8:22). Against this appalling backdrop of
spiritual night, Isaiah proclaimed:

The people who walked in darkness
have seen a great light;
those who dwelt in a land of deep darkness,
on them has light shined (Isa. 9:2).

Perhaps Isaiah was remembering the Shekinah glory
God revealed to his ancestors. When God led the
Israelites out of bondage, he led them by a pillar of fire.
When Moses came down the mountain after his counsel
with God, his face glowed so that the people could not
look upon him. When the temple of Solomon was
dedicated, a radiant cloud filled it. All these instances
revealed the Shekinah glory of God, the radiant light of
his pureness in which no darkness can stand.

However, light not only drives away the darkness but
also reveals the truth. We see things clearly in the light,
and only by the light of Jesus can we ever clearly see
ourselves for what we are. God, who the Psalmist says is
clad "with light as with a garment" (Ps. 104:2), is nothing
to us unless we acknowledge our darkness and seek his
light. Only through the Light of life may we truly see
ourselves.

But once we are brought into God's light, we are one

with him in his radiance. He goes before us, as that light in the desert went before the Israelites, and clearly shows us the way. On that basis, Paul enjoins us, "For once you were darkness, but now you are light in the Lord; walk as children of light" (Eph. 5:8). And John says in his first epistle: "God is light and in him is no darkness at all. If we say we have fellowship with him while we walk in darkness, we lie and do not live according to the truth; but if we walk in the light, as he is in the light, we have fellowship with one another" (1 John 1:5-7). We, like the Light, become lights.

PSALM 4:6

There are many who say, "O that
we might see some good!
Lift up the light of thy countenance
upon us, O Lord!"

PRAYER

O Lord, my Lord,
how majestic is thy name in all the earth!
When I look at thy heavens,
the work of thy fingers,
the moon and the stars which thou
hast established,
what is man that thou art mindful of him?
Yet, you love man so much
that you died for him
to raise those who believe in you
to everlasting life.

TWENTY-SIX
ALPHA AND OMEGA

The name Alpha and Omega has a mystical intrigue for the modern mind that was present among ancient Greek and Hebrew peoples as well. I use the adjectives Greek and Hebrew because both apply to the New Testament, which, for the most part, was written in the Greek language by Hebrew writers. And it was in the New Testament that Jesus received this name. *Alpha and omega* are the first and last letters of the Greek alphabet. Together, they signify the sum, the wholeness, the completion. The equivalents in the Hebrew alphabet are the letters *aleph* and *tau*, which are charged with mystical symbolism perhaps even more than the Greek letters. For example, the Hebrew word for truth is *emeth*, which originally was made up of only three consonants: *aleph*, the first letter from their alphabet; *mem*, the middle letter; and *tau*, the final letter. Since *emeth*, or truth, contains symbolically the beginning, middle, and end, it also stands for God, who contains the entirety of Truth.

While Greek symbolism is not as complex as Hebrew symbolism, it does suggest the eternal nature of God, a truth modern Christians also hold dear. The title Alpha and Omega has become a common one for Jesus in the church today. In our age of rapid change, we treasure the One who is beyond change himself, but in whom all change begins and ends.

Much debate centers on this title, which is given only three times in Scripture, each time in the book of Revelation. Some theologians argue that on each occasion, the title applies to Jesus; others argue that only the third use applies to him. Revelation 1:8 reads: " 'I am the Alpha and the Omega,' says the Lord God, who is and who was and who is to come, the Almighty." Some scholars think that in the context of the preceding verses, this title refers to God the Father. In Revelation 21:6, following the paraphrase from Isaiah 25 that describes specific actions of God the Father, God again declares himself as "The Alpha and the Omega, the beginning and the end." But in Revelation 22:13, the speaker clearly seems to be Jesus (see verse 16) who says, "I am the Alpha and the Omega, the first and the last, the beginning and the end."

The theological debate seems academic when one considers that Jesus is in fact eternal God, one with the Father from all eternity. For Jesus, as for God the Father, a thousand years are but as yesterday. Jesus, with the Father, created all that is. Jesus is the one who will complete history with his return. And in Jesus all is Yea and Amen (2 Cor. 1:20).

This title captures the glory of our eternal Creator and provider. As Alpha and Omega, Jesus transcends temporal affairs because he initiated those affairs. But he is also the One who is immanent, involved hour by hour, day by day, year by year, and age by age in the changing world he has made. Only one who is Alpha and Omega, who holds the beginning and the ending, can be such a God.

Because Jesus is Alpha and Omega, we have an end—a reason for living—as well as a means for living. Paul wrote to the Corinthians, "For us there is one God, the Father, from whom are all things and *for whom we exist,* and one Lord, Jesus Christ, through whom are all things and *through whom we exist"* (1 Cor. 8:6, italics added).

Because Jesus is Alpha and Omega, we have a hope that lies beyond this life. In him we will end our mortal lives to begin anew in eternal life. Paul stated the reason for this hope in his letter to the Colossians:

For in him all the fulness of God was pleased to dwell, and through him to reconcile to himself all things, whether on earth or in heaven, making peace by the blood of his cross (Col. 1:19, 20).

And because Jesus is Alpha and Omega, we have received a new beginning in this life. To know him is to know our end. To know our end in him is to truly begin living for the first time.

2 CORINTHIANS 5:17

Therefore, if any one is in Christ,
he is a new creation;
the old has passed away,
behold, the new has come.

PRAYER

Through your reconciliation of grace, dear Lord,
I am a new creation.
As you wash me with your blood,
I stand clean before my Lord.

TWENTY-SEVEN
PRINCE OF PEACE

Like life itself, and sometimes more than life, mankind craves peace. In moments of terrible honesty, confronted by a dark wall of anxiety and problems, we may all feel that life is not worth living unless we have inner peace.

After seemingly endless months of tossing on the unbroken expanse of the flood, Noah must have longed for the day when he could once again set foot on dry land. A cessation of motion, a time to stand still, a chance to hear a bird's song and see flowers blossom—these must have seemed distant possibilities to him. Yet three times he sent forth a dove to bring a sign that the promise was at hand. The second time, the dove returned with an olive branch, signifying the peaceful end to the storm-tossed journey. Thereby, the symbol of the dove and the olive branch has come to represent peace worldwide. The third time Noah sent forth the dove, it did not return, showing that peace had spread throughout the land.

As an Old Testament sign of simple and blessed peace, it was fitting that the Holy Spirit descended in the form of a dove when John baptized Jesus. The Prince of Peace was at hand.

While the Jews expected the Messiah to come as a

mighty king, an invincible warrior, Jesus came as a bringer of peace. Yet this role had been foretold by the prophets. When Israel was being threatened by Egypt and Assyria, Isaiah prophesied the arrival of a peacemaker, not a military ruler. "His name," said Isaiah, "will be called . . . 'Prince of Peace' " (Isa. 9:6).

Jesus comes as the Prince of Peace, the firstborn of the Lord of all life, and the heir to the title of King of Kings. But while these are his legitimate titles, Prince of Peace also describes the outcome of his reign.

If all people were Christians, there would be no war. But this is not the case, for there is also a prince of darkness roaming this world, and his dark power casts a sword where the Prince of Peace would bring light. Jesus promised that this dark prince would have no power over him—Satan has been defeated at Golgotha— but the evil one has not yet been cast in chains into the fiery lake as he will be at the Second Coming. Until that day, Christians will have to contend with his darkness. But the supreme power belongs to Jesus, for he is, as Revelation 1:5 says, "ruler of kings on earth." His promises are sure.

Zechariah prophesied that his son John would "guide our feet into the way of peace" (Luke 1:79), and that way was made sure when the dove of peace descended upon Jesus. Like Noah's dove, this dove signified a peace that would eventually go out into all the world. Looking forward to his own death, Jesus promised, "Peace I leave with you; my peace I give to you; not as the world gives do I give to you" (John 14:27). His peace is permanent because Jesus is the Prince of Peace, the One whom the darkness cannot overcome. He said, "I have said this to you, that in me you may have peace. In the world you have tribulation; but be of good cheer, I have overcome the world" (John 16:33).

Some of you now reading this huddle in a room with the weight of depression pressing thickly upon you. May the Spirit of Peace fall fresh on you with joy like that first dove. There are some whose lives are twisted with anxiety like a ball of knotted wires ready to burst apart. May the Spirit of Peace fall fresh on you with a calmness that passes understanding. There are some of you who are yourselves, or who have dear ones, battling illnesses that torment and devastate. May the Spirit of Peace fall fresh on you with the far-reaching arm of healing that touched the blind, the sick, the tormented in Galilee and is not shortened in power in our day.

And may all who come to the Prince of Peace unite in the hope expressed so well by the hymnwriter: "My sin— oh, the bliss of this glorious thought—my sin—not in part, but the whole—is nailed to the cross and I bear it no more." By this gift we are made whole and can sing with all our heart: "It is well, it is well with my soul."

PSALM 35:9
My soul shall rejoice in the Lord,
exulting in his deliverance.

PRAYER
O Prince of Peace, God of perfect love,
may your peace fall fresh on me,
and may I bring peace
to those about me.

TWENTY-EIGHT
BREAD OF LIFE:
ONE TRUE SOURCE

For more than ten years, I was the happy resident of small towns. By small, I mean 6,000 inhabitants or less, give or take some stray dogs and occasional passersby who stayed a few days at the Friendly Arms Hotel on Main Street. Many joys accompany small-town life—a leisurely pace, friendly voices, ready companions for a cup of coffee.

By and large, those ten years are filled with happy, if sometimes peculiar, memories. I was fascinated, for example, by the artistic craftsmanship of some of my neighbors. On one road in the Appalachian farmland where I once lived, a farmer skilled at wood carving annually displayed a Christmas crèche hewn out of applewood. Liberally situated in hay, the crèche showed artfully carved oxen, sheep, and magi gathered before a manger in which the farmer had secreted a tiny white light whose glow announced the Light of the World.

I was moved by the display and complimented my neighbor. I looked forward to next year, I told him. So did he. Next year an elaborate, small-scale church appeared behind the stable. It was carefully assembled with miniature stained glass windows, a charming steeple, a full array of interior lights, and fresh white paint that made the whole building rather overwhelm the crèche at its doorstep. Paradoxical? Yes, but not a bad touch, I thought, joining that first Christmas with the modern church. One learns to make the best of things in small towns.

But the next year, also my last there, he produced his masterwork. As always, the crèche was still there. The one tiny light glowed, albeit feebly before the glittering church, which this year had added a string of Christmas lights to its steeple. The church was as pretty as last year. But by a stroke of imagination inspired, no doubt, by malls and catalogs, in its doorway stood a magnificent Santa Claus with a huge feedbag, bulging with packages, draped over one shoulder. A new spotlight bathed the gaudy figure, casting all else—especially the crèche—into shadow.

Another incident comes to mind. I moved from the Appalachian foothills to a small town in western Pennsylvania. It was a bucolic town which, save for automobiles from nearby I-80, seemed never to have progressed past 1950. Despite its cracked sidewalks, its curious blend of the archaic and the merely old, I loved the place. And my neighbors.

All seemed well that first year. Christmas was jovial, and if Santas slightly outnumbered crèches, they at least appeared in separate yards.

Nothing prepared me, then, for the following Easter. The house at the corner of Craig and Garden Streets stood atop a hill visible for some distance. It had three large white pillars supporting a front porch. On Easter morning, as I walked to a sunrise service on the football field, I noticed with some horror that the owner had decorated the pillars with sprigs of yew and purple ribbons and three large forms, one hung on each pillar. The figures on the two outside pillars were slightly smaller than the central figure, which was nearly six feet high. As I walked closer to the house, I affirmed what I didn't want to believe. Each of the figures was a large, stuffed Easter bunny.

I didn't know whether to chuckle or weep. Perhaps a person does the one only to prevent the other. But this much is clear to me: each of my two neighbors had wanted to be all things to all men. And each had wound up with precisely nothing.

Each had, if you will, traded bread for silver and gone hungry.

ISAIAH 55:2, 3

Why do you spend your money
for that which is not bread,
and your labor for that which does not satisfy?
Hearken diligently to me,
and eat what is good,
and delight yourselves in fatness.
Incline your ear, and come to me;
hear, that your soul may live.

PRAYER

Lord, Judas traded your life for pieces of silver.
Hold me back, Lord, from that bad bargain.
May all my hunger be for the true Bread of Life.

TWENTY-NINE
BREAD OF LIFE: DIETARY STAPLE

And still we trade bread for silver, bartering the simple truth which Jesus brought for something fancier, gaudier, more resplendent.

Little is known about the forty days Jesus was tempted in the wilderness by Satan. The biblical account of this important event is rendered objectively and sparingly. Yet what a significant event. Here, at the start of Jesus' ministry, was a crossroads—the way of the world or the way to the cross. And once the choice was made, there would be no turning back. To Jesus, Satan offered the way of the world—a lucrative, compelling world paved with power and wealth.

One of the temptations may have been prompted by the very geography of the land. From the mountaintop where Jesus and Satan stood, the tumbled rocks in the valley far below looked, in fact, like small loaves of bread. Remember that Jesus had been fasting as Satan said, "If you are the Son of God, command these stones to become loaves of bread" (Matt. 4:3).

A world of meaning lies in this temptation, for it appeals not just to Jesus' great hunger but to the hungry everywhere. Imagine that all those stones were to become bread. There would be enough of this universal staple to feed hungry people everywhere. As bread-giver, Jesus would earn the people's puppet-like dependence upon him. He would be a feudal lord.

But this temptation confronted the Son of God who had, in fact, created bread already—not out of stones, but out of nothing—when he fed the Israelites manna in the desert. Puppetlike subservience from those who received bread was not called for then, nor is it called for now. Rather, God desires our obedient worship—worship due the One who is able to provide for our *every* need.

To fully appreciate Satan's temptation, one must understand the significance of bread as a dietary staple in Jesus' day. The word bread was so diverse in meaning in the Jewish nation that it could apply to all kinds of food in addition to the common flour base—usually wheat or barley—loaf. In many larger towns, there were public ovens for baking bread. In smaller villages, the dough was often baked over a pit in an open room. Other modes of baking included pans, heated stones, and heated sand of ash pits. Making bread was an important daily ritual.

Along with the dietary significance of bread lay a religious and figurative significance. Since the time of the Exodus, bread figured prominently into worship services as a sign of God's presence and communion with his people. On this basis, Jesus celebrated the Passover with his disciples, a feast to which he gave specifically Christian meaning by claiming that the bread and wine were his body and blood. This we now commemorate, according to Jesus' invitation, in the Lord's Supper.

In resisting Satan's temptation, Jesus, in effect, did two things. First, he freed people to worship him rather than be his slaves. But second, he went on to give them life in himself. He later proclaimed, in what must have been a thoroughly startling claim to his audience, "I am the bread of life. He who comes to me shall not hunger" (John 6:35).

Here is the breathtaking truth: When we give Jesus our worship, he, in turn, gives us the bread of life—both literally and figuratively. He will watch over his children providing for their staple needs, their daily bread. But more important, he gives us life eternal. We will enjoy God's presence forever.

Some people are bent on trading bread for silver. They would give up their sure and staple diet for the elusive, passing charms that strut across the stage of this world. Job said that wisdom "cannot be gotten for gold, and silver cannot be weighed as its price" (Job 28:15). The truly wise will seek the bread of life that Jesus, Bread of Life, offers in his body and in his blood.

1 JOHN 5:12
He who has the Son has life;
he who has not the Son of God has not life.

PRAYER
With your disciples,
in those last days,
you broke bread and said,
"This is my body."
By invitation of your eternal Word,
which is sure and true,
I, too, join in partaking of your bread of life.

THIRTY
TRUE VINE

One is amazed how over and over Jesus refers to the
most common tasks and affairs of men. Nothing seems to
escape his notice. His examples are often simple, yet they
cut through the flurry of issues to the very heart of truth.
Would you talk about who gives the most to the
kingdom? Let's consider the widow's mite. Would you
discuss the sin of drunkenness? Let's remember the
prodigal son. Do you have great needs? Let's consider the
sparrow. So it is with the names Jesus gives himself; they
speak of everyday realities.

Why is this? Why does Jesus identify himself in the
simple terms of common, daily life?

Jesus is not foremost a subject for theologians; he is
foremost a man among men, the divine touch on the
humblest stations of humanity, the light of God in the
smallest, most dismal corner of life. Jesus lives theology
in the church of daily life. He is not a rabbi of the
synagogue; he is Rabboni among the people.

Some titles of Jesus bespeak his great glory. Bright
Morning Star is a majestic name, thundering across the
vast stretches of spiritual night in unalterable light. Alpha
and Omega testifies to the perfect divinity of Jesus; he is

the One who began all that is, and he is the One in whom all is fulfilled. But then we have a name like the True Vine, and we see Jesus once again among the people.

"I am the true vine. . . . you are the branches," Jesus says to his disciples (John 15:1, 5). But why the vine? It is easy for us to picture the cornerstone of a building, and when Jesus says he is the cornerstone of the church, we immediately intuit that our faith is built on him. But the vine? Did he choose this image because wine was a common drink of the Jewish nation? Because wine was a communal drink for mealtimes and the passing of the cup suggested unity?

Surely these are good points to consider. But let us look further. The vine was not a particularly admired or noble plant in Palestine. In fact, it seldom had the elaborate support systems of fences and arches we now use in modern vineyards. It often ran wild, trailing in the dust or sprawling on hillsides, or was supported by nothing more than sticks or rude trellises at best. Most likely, Jesus purposely linked himself not to the noblest plant—say, the cedar or the olive—but to the most common and humble.

Surprisingly, Israel, God's chosen nation, often is spoken of in the Old Testament as a vine. Several times, Ezekiel describes Israel as a once splendid vine now grown useless and good for nothing (Ezek. 15:1-8; 19:10-14). To bear fruit, vineyards need to be tended carefully. Ezekiel shows that, despite God's tender care, Israel willfully allows itself to sprawl into ruin. Ruin is also the subject of Isaiah's parable (Isa. 5:1-7). And Jeremiah states it more directly:

Yet I planted you a choice vine,
wholly of pure seed.
How then have you turned degenerate
and become a wild vine? (Jer. 2:21).

When Jesus speaks at length in John 15 about his nature as the True Vine, he is describing himself as a new vine from which the true church may be built. His people, he says, are branches of the True Vine. We take our very lives from being grafted into him, and his life pours into us. This graft is made and nourished, says Jesus, by the Father, who is the vinedresser.

Wild vineyards bear no fruit. But branches of the True Vine, which are the new church of Jesus' redeemed, bear fruit. By virtue of being grafted into Christ, his fruits— the fruits of the Spirit—are poured into us for nourishment. He provides the very lifeblood of the Christian church. But we also bear fruit as tangible evidence of our new position in Jesus. Any branches that fail to do so are pruned away.

Above all, this name for Jesus, with its image of us being grafted into him, offers great security. As his life pours into us, the grafted branches, we become one with him, the main vine. What is the vine without its fruit-bearing branches? Who can say where the branch begins and the vine ends? This name emphasizes our oneness, our unity, with Jesus in much the same way that the passing of the cup at his last supper emphasized Jesus' unity with his disciples.

MATTHEW 26:27, 28
Drink of it, all of you;
for this is my blood of the covenant,
which is poured out for many
for the forgiveness of sins.

PRAYER
Thank you, Jesus,
for the forgiveness

you have offered me,
for the commemoration
that I am grafted into your body,
the one True Vine.

THIRTY-ONE
SON OF GOD, SON OF MAN

After a careful study of the New Testament, no one can doubt Jesus' claim to divinity. Among the first to pay homage to him as the Son of God were the demons. In the synagogue at Capernaum, a man possessed by a demon cried out, "Ah! What have you to do with us, Jesus of Nazareth? Have you come to destroy us? I know who you are, the Holy One of God" (Luke 4:34). Later, the two Gadarene demoniacs shouted, "What have you to do with us, O Son of God?" (Matt. 8:29). And during his temptation of Jesus in the wilderness, Satan, the father of demons, openly referred to Jesus as the Son of God (Matt. 4:3, 5).

There were other times, of course, when Jesus' divine title is made clear. For example, the Holy Spirit announced Jesus' divinity at his baptism (Luke 3:22). When Jesus walked on the water to Peter, Peter exclaimed, "Truly, you are the Son of God" (Matt. 14:33). Jesus himself spoke of doing his Father's will (John 6:38-40). There can be no question from these passages that Jesus' Father is God himself. That Jesus is the Son of God is the overwhelming theme of other New Testament books as well.

And well it should be, for this is the heart of
Christianity: The Son of God became flesh and dwelt
among us (John 1:14). For us, this is an unfathomable
truth. Why should one give up the glories of heaven to
live as a man and to die like a criminal—worse, to die for
crimes not his?

But reverse the perspective. For the Son of God, the
truly remarkable thing must have been to become man.
Thus, it is not surprising that Jesus names himself over
and over the Son of Man. The title is used more than
sixty times in the synoptic Gospels and several times in
the Gospel of John. Outside of the Gospels, which, of
course, concern themselves with the life of Jesus, the
name is used only a few times. One of those is in Acts,
where Stephen says, "I can see the Son of man standing
at the right hand of God" (Acts 7:55). But Jesus calls
himself the Son of Man repeatedly, reinforcing another
marvelous truth: The Messiah, the Son of God, is fully
man.

But why the title, Son of Man? Precisely because all
that Jesus does and all that he means is present in *himself*,
in his bodily form. In fact, Jesus uses the title when he is
making some of his greatest claims for himself.

As Son of Man, he is the *redeemer:* "For the Son of
man came to seek and to save the lost" (Luke 19:10).
And also, "For the Son of man also came not to be served
but to serve, and to give his life as a ransom for many"
(Mark 10:45).

As Son of Man, he is *resurrected* from the dead, having
paved a way redeemed man may follow. To Martha, Jesus
said, "I am the resurrection and the life; he who believes
in me, though he die, yet shall he live, and whoever lives
and believes in me shall never die" (John 11:25, 26).

As Son of Man, he has *ascended* and prepared a place
for those who will be resurrected to be with him: "I tell
you, hereafter you will see the Son of Man seated at the
right hand of Power, and coming on the clouds of
heaven" (Matt. 26:64).

And, finally, as Son of Man, he will *return again:* "For the Son of man is to come with his angels in the glory of his Father, and then he will repay every man for what he has done" (Matt. 16:27).

None of these events is possible unless Jesus became the Son of Man. The true glory lies here: The Son of God became Son of Man to redeem the lost, to resurrect the redeemed, to ascend and prepare a place in glory, and to return again to judge the world.

ROMANS 5:17

If, because of one man's trespass,
death reigned through that one man,
much more will those who receive
the abundance of grace and the free gift
of righteousness reign in life
through the one man Jesus Christ.

PRAYER

Lord, as the words of a song proclaim,
"You left the splendor of heaven
knowing your destiny
was the lonely hill of Golgotha,
There to lay down your life for me."
For your unfailing love, I thank you.

THIRTY-TWO
MESSIAH: PROMISED ONE

In C. S. Lewis's well-known story, *The Lion, the Witch and the Wardrobe*, four English children find themselves in the fantasy world of Narnia. This Narnia is encased in a frigid winter that has endured a hundred winters without a thaw. The White Witch has placed her spell on the land, enslaving it to a climate as hard and cold as her own cruel nature. The worst thing, however, is that it is always winter and never Christmas. One can imagine the joy of the Narnians when, after a hundred years of unrelenting expectation, Father Christmas finally arrives.

The fantasy world of always winter but never Christmas may seem quite unlike our own world. With the commercialization of Christmas into an eight- to ten-week sell-a-thon, it almost seems as if it's always Christmas—even before winter arrives. One wearies of seeing the great Advent reduced to mere adventure in toy shops. We wonder, "How much earlier can they make it?" and then each year stand amazed as stores and malls step up the Christmas advertising just a few days earlier. In the race for the dollar, after all, Christmas runs well.

It may merit our reflection to consider God's earliest Christmas, for we find it already promised in the Book of Genesis at the dawn of history.

God's clean, new world was hardly made when sin wriggled into it like a vicious blot. What a smear on the canvas of beauty! Imagine an artist laboring over a beautiful landscape painting, a painting so full it ripples with life—birds in feathered raiment, fish sparkling in silver waters, animals at play in gardens and forests. And when at last the artist finishes, imagine someone cruelly slashing the painting so that the original is irrevocably marred. This is but a pale representation of the wound in God's living creation when sin entered the world.

One might expect God, standing before the blighted ruins of his perfect artistry, to rage against sin. Since he is perfectly just, God must exact retribution. Every sin has its price. But here at the very dawn of time, God responds instead by wishing his people the earliest Merry Christmas. One shall come, he says, who will bear the full terror of the penalty for their sin. In Genesis 3:15, God promises to the temptation-bringing serpent:

I will put enmity between you and the woman,
and between your seed and her seed;
he shall bruise your head,
and you shall bruise his heel.

A future offspring in the lineage of this first woman Eve, a child born to human parents, will somehow crush the serpent's head while bearing the serpent's sting. God looks across the centuries and sees his son, Jesus, on the cross.

Yes, the serpent shall bruise Jesus' heel. The sting of sin, the weight of our stripes, and the burden of our iniquities will be upon him there on the cross. But through this cross, Jesus will defeat Satan. He will bear Satan's sting, and his blood will pay the penalty for our sins. The crushing blow to Satan's head, the death blow, is freedom from sin through the redemption of Jesus.

And there in the scarred garden, when by all rights

God's wrath could be kindled, in love and kindness beyond imagination he wishes us the earliest Merry Christmas. The unspeakable gift of his Son, Jesus, will bring our winter of sin to an end.

1 JOHN 4:9, 10

In this the love of God was made manifest among us,
that God sent his only Son into the world,
so that we might live through him.
In this is love, not that we loved God
but that he loved us and sent his Son
to be the expiation for our sins.

PRAYER

This indeed is love, Lord:
that Jesus came and dwelt among men.
When the angels sang hallelujah,
Glory to the newborn king,
few rejoiced on earth; shepherds,
wisemen, Joseph and Mary and their relation.
But how that song of rejoicing,
that glorious hallelujah has spread.
My song of praise joins in: Glory, hallelujah
to the newborn king.

THIRTY-THREE
MESSIAH:
EXPECTED ONE

The Christmas story of Jesus' incarnation, the story J. I. Packer calls "love to the uttermost for unlovely men," is the fulfillment of God's persistent mercy toward his people. In *Knowing God* (Downers Grove: InterVarsity, 1979), Packer elaborates:

The Christmas message is that there is hope for a ruined humanity—hope of pardon, hope of peace with God, hope of glory—because at the Father's will Jesus Christ became poor, and was born in a stable so that thirty years later He might hang on a cross. It is the most wonderful message the world has ever heard, or will hear.

It is little wonder the Christian world looks forward to the celebration of Christmas with excitement. But think back to God's first Merry Christmas announcement in Genesis 3:15. How the ancient people must have looked forward to Jesus' coming. The problem is they already had defined to the Giver the gift they wanted; their Messiah conformed to *their* shopping list. When the real Messiah appeared, they didn't even recognize him.

Their blindness was not for a lack of adequate signs. Over and over, God sent signs and wonders directing

people to the One who was to come. The voices of the
prophets seemed to rise in agonized chorus. Isaiah cried
out, "Hear, you deaf; and look, you blind, that you may
see" (Isa. 42:18). The signs were all about. The prophecies
abundantly pointed to a coming Savior.

Even people, such as David, foreshadowed the coming
Christ. Like Jesus, David's kingship is ordained by God
and his rule, in a small way, imitates Jesus' reign. David's
psalms bear ample evidence of his concern for the coming
Redeemer.

But nowhere, perhaps, is the foreshadowing more
powerful than in the characters of Abraham and Isaac.
One often wonders whether the grim scene enacted on
Moriah is only a test of Abraham's faith, or whether it is
a wondrous sign from God to his people—a sign that
shows God's intervening grace and his willingness to bear
the sacrificial burden. The episode in Genesis 22 would
seem to be a startling testimony to the latter.

God calls Abraham to take his *only* son to Moriah, a
journey of three days. In a sense, the death of Isaac is
certain on the first day, the day of departure. On the third
day, at Moriah, Isaac is lifted from the sentence of death.
Abraham is called by faith alone; only by absolute
obedience to the word of God can he see this grim trial
through. Yet Abraham believes; he goes forth.

When they arrive at Moriah, the aged Abraham is
forced by his infirmity to lay the wood of the sacrificial
offering upon the back of Isaac. This lamb, too, had to
bear the full burden of the sacrifice, just as that later
Lamb would bear his own cross on the way to Golgotha.

Still Abraham goes forth in obedience and in faith. One
imagines he experiences terrible dread, for he loves Isaac
deeply. But he loves God more.

As they ascend the mountain, Abraham has only this to
say to Isaac: "God will provide himself the lamb for a
burnt offering, my son" (Gen. 22:8). What more can he
say? He holds the fire and the knife!

Did Abraham know what was to come? Could he know that God's angel would intervene in the split second before the downward plunge of his knife? Of course not. But he believed; he had faith. In what? That God would provide, surely. But this passage, with its emphasis in the original Hebrew, says, "God will provide *himself!*"

Here is the great foreshadowing, for God himself bore our burden on the cross—God in the person of *his* dearly beloved Son Jesus. Abraham left the place, giving it a name of promise that pointed to the Messiah—the Lord will provide—since "On the mount of the Lord it *shall* be provided" (Gen. 22:14, emphasis added).

This the Messiah did. He is God's provision for all mankind, which longs anxiously for the greatest Christmas gift of all.

GALATIANS 3:6, 7
Thus Abraham "believed God, and it was reckoned
to him as righteousness."
So you see it is men of faith
who are the sons of Abraham.

PRAYER
Lord, my righteousness rests
in your supreme gift.
Thank you, Jesus, for the gift of life
in your perfect sacrifice.

THIRTY-FOUR
MESSIAH:
DESCENDANT OF DAVID

Jesus comes as the fulfillment of Old Testament
expectation, and that expectation almost always focused
on the office of the Messiah. Perhaps no other title of
Jesus is richer in its implications to the Hebrew nation or
dearer in its fulfillment to the Christian church.

Sometimes we fail to realize how thoroughly we have
incorporated the title of Messiah into our Christian life.
The Hebrew word *Messiah* means simply "the anointed
one." In the Gospels, the Hebrew word is given its Greek
equivalent, *"Christos,"* or "Christ." Thus, every time we
speak or think of Jesus as Christ we are, in effect,
referring to Jesus as Messiah. It would be interesting to
count the number of times the title Christ is used in just
one worship service. Each time, the word may as well be
Messiah.

The messianic nature of Jesus, then, is a profound and
living aspect of the Christ we worship. As Jesus was, so
he is, and so he continues to be in the future. What are
the roots of the title Messiah, or Christ?

From the earliest passages of the Old Testament to the
last, the idea of a Messiah is expressed. In its early stages,
the concept is largely that of a deliverer with a prophetic

role—one who would clearly and truthfully relate God's will. With the establishment of the kings over Israel, however, the title takes on a distinctly royal, authoritative bearing. It is particularly associated with the lineage of David.

A subtle historical point intrudes here. We recall it was the people of Israel who demanded a king to rule over them. They wanted to be "like all the nations" (1 Sam. 8:5). When Samuel intercedes with God, the Lord makes it clear that "they have not rejected you, but they have rejected me from being king over them" (1 Sam. 8:7). This is a key point: Saul, the king approved by the people, represents the people's rejection of God as their king. God gave them what they wanted. Saul was outstanding, tall, handsome—a king that met the people's criteria. But the Messiah will be *God's* choice, and once again, God will rule his people.

Why did God select the lineage of David for the future Messiah? Because David, unlike Saul, was God's choice of a replacement. Jesse, David's father, didn't even think it worthwhile to call David in from the fields to meet Samuel. This young shepherd couldn't be king! This humble lad! Yet, this is God's choice—not the popular star who stands head and shoulders above others, but the humble shepherd. God will work through whomever he will.

We never forget, of course, that David was not the Messiah but merely a human king. His reign is wracked by sin and sorrow. Still, as God's anointed, King David exemplified many traits that would also mark the Messiah to come.

First, David showed great mercy, not only on the poor and oppressed, but even on his enemies. Several times the life of Saul lay in David's hand, and he refused to squeeze it out.

Second, David was a worshipful king who sought, through his own human frailty, to honor the God who chose him. The Psalms in particular bear eloquent witness to David's respect for God.

Third, David sought justice in his kingdom. Though his sinful, human nature led him to commit unjust acts, David was keenly aware of the times he violated God's standards, and he labored to rule as a fair king.

In these ways David suggests—but only suggests—the identity of the Messiah who was to come and rule as king.

1 JOHN 3:23

And this is his commandment,
that we should believe in the name
of his Son Jesus Christ and love one another,
just as he has commanded us.

PRAYER

As John says in his first epistle,
"God is greater than our hearts."
It is by God in my heart that I can say,
"Jesus is the Messiah, Lord of all."

THIRTY-FIVE
LION OF JUDAH

In his *Chronicles of Narnia*, C. S. Lewis portrays the great lion Aslan as the king and creator of Narnia. Because he is the creator of Narnia, Aslan is also its king. No made thing can be greater than its Maker. As God said through the prophet Isaiah: "Does the clay say to him who fashions it, 'What are you making'? Or, 'Your work has no handles'?" (Isa. 45:9). No created thing queries its creator.

As the creator of Narnia, Aslan rules the land with absolute authority. When the Pevensie children first hear of Aslan, they understandably question, "But is he safe?" Their guide, Mr. Beaver, responds that, of course, he is safe—but he's not *tame*. Aslan is safe. He can be depended upon to act according to his royal and revealed nature. But he is not tame. One cannot place him in a pocket and domesticate him to act as one wishes.

The kingship of Jesus, like Aslan's, finds its roots in his nature as Creator. Jesus is fully man, but he is also fully God. As God is the Creator, so is Jesus. This important fact precedes all talk about his kingship. Scriptural passages may declare and describe Jesus' kingship, but their descriptions are based on Jesus' very nature. He is king before any man calls him king. His position does not depend upon human recognition, nor upon winning an election. His is an anointed office—anointed by God the Father from all eternity.

Matthew and Luke are careful in their gospels to trace Jesus' genealogy in the Davidic line by way of demonstrating his messiahship. Yet Jesus himself rejects this emphasis:

How can the scribes say that the Christ is the son of David?
David himself, inspired by the Holy Spirit, declared,
  "The Lord said to my Lord,
  Sit at my right hand,
  till I put thy enemies under thy feet."
David himself calls him Lord; so how is he his son? (Mark
12:35-37)

Jesus is not a lately ascended king. He is king—at once and forever.

To help us consider the unique qualities of Jesus' kingship, we might look at the Bible's curious and surprising association of the lion, the king of beasts, with the King of Man. In the Old Testament, this association is a frequent one.

The regality, nobility, and power of the lion are commonly noted facts in the Old Testament. God himself asks Job, "Can you hunt the prey for the lion, or satisfy the appetite of the young lions?" (Job 38:39). Frequently, the lion is associated with a ruling authority, as in Proverbs 19:12, "A king's wrath is as the growling of a lion."

Through the words of the prophet Jeremiah, God likens himself to the lion: "Behold, like a lion coming up from the jungle of the Jordan against a strong sheepfold, I will suddenly make them run away from her; and I will appoint over her whomever I choose" (Jer. 49:19). In Hosea, God compares himself to the lion—this time with reference to his rule over his chosen people: "For I will be like a lion to Ephraim, and like a young lion to the house of Judah" (Hos. 5:14). Hosea 11:10 repeats the theme:

They shall go after the Lord,
he will roar like a lion;
yea, he will roar,
and his sons shall come trembling. . . .

The Old Testament image of the lion as the king of his people and the New Testament image of Jesus merge in Revelation 5:5, where Jesus is described specifically as "the Lion of the tribe of Judah, the Root of David." John has been weeping because not one of all the magnificent angelic creatures he has seen has the worth or inherent authority to open the Book of Life. The elder comforts him: There is One who has the necessary kingly authority, and it is Jesus.

The offspring of royal lineage, the root of David, and the King of all the redeemed merge in the one Jesus who alone is worthy to open the book of eternal life. The song of joy that bursts on John's ears is a ringing testimony: "To him who sits upon the throne and to the Lamb be blessing and honor and glory and might for ever and ever!" (Rev. 5:13).

HEBREWS 2:9
But we see Jesus,
who for a little while was made lower than the angels,
crowned with glory and honor
because of the suffering of death,
so that by the grace of God
he might taste death for every one.

PRAYER
With the angels and the redeemed of all the ages,
I proclaim glory and honor and power
to the King of Kings: Crown him Lord of all.

THIRTY-SIX
SERVANT

In John's glorious revelation, the Lion of the tribe of Judah, the Root of David, is announced as the One who is worthy to open the Book of Life (Rev. 5:5). Since he has conquered death upon the cross and in his resurrection, Jesus alone can open the Book of Life. But when he is announced, who comes forward?

We see not a majestic king in royal robes, but a lamb whose royalty is inherent. Biblically, two ideas are associated with the lamb—first, the suffering servant, and second, the perfect sacrifice. Consider the servant first.

Can the King of Kings be a servant also? Can the perfect ruler and absolute authority also be the perfectly ruled and perfectly obedient?

The idea of the suffering servant in the Old Testament is always one of a man who suffers unjustly and undeservedly. His suffering seems to be not for his own crime but for the crimes of others. The concept is most clearly expressed in Isaiah 53, which describes the One who will bear our griefs and burdens.

In our age, we might be tempted to call such a person a fool. Indeed, the idea of someone who willingly suffers for others seems a complete perversion of our standards of justice. We believe the guilty party should be punished, the innocent exonerated.

But curiously, we also find in our time similar portraits of such selfless love. We see a person share others' burdens to such an extent that we can only stand amazed and speak of his nobility, love, and servanthood. Mother Teresa walks the squalid streets of India, touching tormented lives with human kindness, and we shake our heads in disbelief. Dr. Peter Boelens, Director of the Luke Society, uses his medical talents in the Philippines, in leper colonies, in Haiti, in devastated areas of the Mississippi Delta, and often his only thanks is a sigh of relief.

The point here is that the suffering servant is not *servile.* He is neither weak nor a fool. The suffering servant has a fixed purpose—willful obedience—and a huge strength to accomplish it.

To think of Jesus as the suffering servant, as one "stricken, smitten by God, and afflicted . . . wounded for our transgressions . . . bruised for our iniquities (Is. 53:4, 5), is to think of Jesus as *obedient,* not as *servile.*

There is this difference about Jesus, however. As the perfectly obedient One who is at once the perfectly righteous One, he bears our sins to wipe them away. He accomplishes what no mere human can accomplish.

The Old Testament portrait of the suffering servant is emphatically echoed by the New Testament. One of the most startling pictures is in Acts where Philip meets the Ethiopian eunuch on the road to Gaza. The Ethiopian is studying the passage we have just quoted from Isaiah 53. He asks Philip to guide his understanding of the passage. "Then Philip opened his mouth, and beginning with this scripture he told him the good news of Jesus" (Acts 8:35).

Several times in the New Testament, Jesus is called the servant. But more significantly, he *was* the servant—not just by bending to wash the disciples' feet, to which one of them remonstrated, "Lord, do you wash my feet?"

(John 13:6), but by bending to the weight of our sins on the cross. By his stripes we are made whole.

MATTHEW 6:24

No one can serve two masters;
for either he will hate the one and love the other,
or he will be devoted to the one and despise the other.
You cannot serve God and mammon.

PRAYER

Often in this life I seem to wear myself out in servility.
There are demands upon my time, my energy,
my sense of humor, my peacefulness.
Then I think of you,
willing to serve even to the cross,
and I pray that you will transform my servility
to a service of praise.

THIRTY-SEVEN
LAMB OF GOD

The Lamb comes with the humility of the suffering servant, but also with the authority of the One who has conquered sin and its consequences. Because he was willing to set aside his royal throne and bear the burden of a fallen mankind, this Lamb, Jesus the Messiah, is the perfect sacrifice.

The idea of the sacrificial lamb was perhaps as thoroughly engrained in the ancient Jewish mind as the Lord's Supper is engrained in ours. The sacrifice was an important event for the Jewish nation. Not just any lamb could be offered to the Lord. Special qualities needed to distinguish it. As early as the giving of the law to Moses, God made several characteristics clear.

First, the animal had to be from the *best* of the flock. Second, it could have no blemish or spot. This requirement was reaffirmed often in the Old Testament: in Exodus 12:5 ("your lamb shall be without blemish"), Leviticus 9:2, 3, and Numbers 29:2. The lamb needed to be without blemish because, third, it was offered to the holy and perfect One, God Almighty. The sacrifice was directed from man to the throne of God's grace, and no defect can stand in his presence.

In each sacrifice, however, the lamb stood in place of man and acted as a substitute for man's sin. Only an unblemished creature could bear the sins of another.

In a curious variation of the offering of the lamb, we have the important Old Testament ritual of the scapegoat. The goat was designated as the specific bearer of sin in a ritual described in Leviticus 16. The priest, Aaron, would lay his hands on the head of the goat in a symbolic transfer of sin: "Aaron shall lay both his hands upon the head of the live goat, and confess over him all the iniquities of the people of Israel, and all their transgressions, all their sins; and he shall put them upon the head of the goat, and send him away into the wilderness . . ." (Lev. 16:21). The scapegoat bore on his body the sins of the people.

These two events—the sacrifice of the lamb without blemish and the transfer of sins to a scapegoat—merge in Jesus. When John the Baptist sees Jesus and proclaims, "Behold, the Lamb of God, who takes away the sin of the world" (John 1:29), he announces the Messiah, who alone can do perfectly the task that the Old Testament rituals only pointed to. This is the perfect Lamb, the One without blemish sent from God, who takes away the sins of all who believe in him. In him alone is forgiveness of sin.

Unlike the Old Testament rituals, which had to be exercised over and over again, Jesus' fulfillment of God's requirements was for all time. In his first letter, Peter points out the completeness of Jesus' redemption. You know, writes Peter, that you are ransomed "with the precious blood of Christ, like that of a lamb without blemish or spot. He was destined before the foundation of the world . . ." (1 Pet. 1:19, 20).

Christina Rossetti gave this great truth special poignancy in her poem, "None Other Lamb":

None other Lamb, none other Name,
  None other Hope in heaven or earth or sea,

None other Hiding-place from guilt and shame,
  None beside thee.

Jesus provided the perfect sacrifice, for he alone was the perfect Lamb. By him, we learn in Revelation 13:8, our names are written in the Book of Life. But although he gave himself to be slain, the Lamb of God was resurrected and now reigns as the perfect Messiah: "They will make war on the Lamb, and the Lamb will conquer them, for he is Lord of lords and King of kings, and those with him are called and chosen and faithful" (Rev. 17:14).

JEREMIAH 29:11-14

For I know the plans I have for you, says the Lord,
plans for welfare and not for evil,
to give you a future and a hope.
Then you will call upon me and come and pray to me,
and I will hear you.
You will seek me and find me:
when you seek me with all your heart,
I will be found by you, says the Lord.

PRAYER

Often I wonder, what can I bring him
who has given everything?
Only this: my life laid before him—
not as a sacrifice on the altar,
for he has given himself as the perfect sacrifice—
but as an act of thanksgiving and praise.

THIRTY-EIGHT
HIGH PRIEST

In the Old Testament, the lamb was sacrificed under the authority of the priest. But what priest had enough authority to sacrifice the Lamb of God himself? Only he who gave himself as the perfect sacrifice: Jesus.

The priests were a special people set apart by God to mediate between God and man. As a sign of the special position they filled, the priests, like Jesus, were anointed to their task.

Consider why the Old Testament people needed a priest. It was a terrible and frightening thing for fallen man to approach the most high and holy God. The sweet communion Adam and Eve shared with God in Eden was replaced by an unbridgeable gulf created by sin. No person could cross the chasm by his own virtue. Only God could provide a bridge. That bridge became the priest, a position God created out of his immeasurable grace and love.

God appointed the priest to be an intercessor for the people. But so powerful is the very presence of God that even the appointed high priest could enter the Holy of Holies, the place where God's presence came to rest, only one day of the year, on the Day of Atonement. The chasm sin created was simply too great for man to bridge.

But Jesus, as we have seen, provided himself as the perfect sacrifice. Since his sacrifice is complete in every way, since the debt of man is finished (as Jesus said on the cross), and since no further debt must be paid, Jesus now and forever bridges the gulf between man and God. He officiates as the High Priest, the mediator by whom we can come into the presence of God without fear. On this basis, the author of Hebrews can say, "Let us then with confidence draw near to the throne of grace" (Heb. 4:16). Jesus, fully God and a "priest forever" (Heb. 5:6), intercedes for us.

In the fifth chapter of Hebrews, this perfect High Priest is carefully described. We learn he acts on behalf of men and has provided the sacrifice that allows men into God's presence (Heb. 5:1). We learn, secondly, that this High Priest Jesus is not a stern or despising ruler, but a gentle and loving guide (Heb. 5:2). We learn, thirdly, that Jesus is called by God, that he acts with God's full authority, that as he acts so God acts (Heb. 5:4). In comparison to earlier priests, the writer adds, Jesus provides "a better hope . . . through which we draw near to God" (Heb. 7:19).

Unlike the priests of the Jewish nation—priests who were mortal and fallen, priests who had to issue sacrifice after sacrifice in wearying succession—Jesus arrives as the perfection of priesthood. Not only did he *come to us* to bear the full horror of our sins, but he now stands *for us* "at the right hand of the throne of the Majesty in heaven, a minister in the sanctuary and the true tent which is set up not by man but by the Lord" (Heb. 8:1, 2).

The anointed One, who is our King but who made himself our Servant, who is both Lion and Lamb, Ruler and Redeemer, is now also our Advocate at the eternal throne of grace.

HEBREWS 9:24
For Christ has entered,
not into a sanctuary made with hands,
a copy of the true one,
but into heaven itself,
now to appear in the presence of God on our behalf.

PRAYER
Since you are the perfect Priest,
I have need of no other intercessor
save you, Jesus.
I bring to you only myself,
knowing that you have already received me
and have paved the way for me.

THIRTY-NINE
KING

If we are children of God, says Paul in his letter to the Romans, we are "heirs of God and fellow heirs with Christ" (Rom. 8:17). No longer is the Holy of Holies closed to us; through Jesus we now live in the continual presence of God.

We have become royal citizens of his kingdom.

We may wonder why, in John 18.36, Jesus rejected an earthly kingship when he so clearly fulfilled the royal title. The Jewish nation had looked forward to the Messiah. He would be king and redeemer. He would bring freedom because he brought security. He would bring justice because he would be the worthy judge.

But if Jesus had accepted this crown, how much would have been lost! To accept the temporal crown would have prevented the bestowal of the eternal crown. Jesus would have been but one more king who, for a time, instituted a just reign on earth. But Jesus is not one more king; he is King from all time, for all time, throughout all time. He reigns as eternal King.

What is the nature of his kingdom, then? Do we merely travel through this world until we die and are resurrected into his eternal realm?

The marvelous response is that as Jesus dwelt among men, so his kingdom dwells among men. The kingdom of God is with us now, in this life. In Jesus' own words: "The time is fulfilled, and the kingdom of God is at hand" (Mark 1:15). Again, in John 17:3, Jesus says, "This is eternal life, that they know thee the only true God, and Jesus Christ whom thou hast sent." If this is the case, then at the moment we confess Jesus in this life, we enter his eternal kingdom. And once we enter it, "who shall separate us from the love of Christ?" (Rom. 8:35).

Where is God's kingdom, then? Mark 1:15 certainly seems to indicate it was present from the moment of Jesus' birth, but it has a future aspect as well. "It will come in power," says Jesus in Mark 9:1. It seems that although we are in the kingdom now, it has not yet fully arrived.

If we choose to walk in the kingdom of God in this life as well as in eternal life—and the two are separated only by death—then our walk in this life will be characterized by certain traits. If we would follow in the footsteps of Jesus, we must serve as he served. If we are ruled by the Messiah who saved us, we will live in obedience to that Messiah. If we accept Jesus as Savior, we necessarily accept him as Lord.

Many traits of our walk in the kingdom of God may be inferred from the walk of Jesus himself. Like him, for example, we will be merciful—even to those who despitefully use us. We will bear one another's burdens, reaching out to the lonely and the lost. We will not sit back and expect to be waited upon. We will live at peace with God's creation, reverencing plants and woods and flowers and skies and seas. We will respect animals. We will share our resources with others. We will strive for justice even when we are accused unjustly.

All these individual qualities may be summarized in Jesus' great injunction to love one another. The password of the kingdom is captured in one word, *agape*—a love for the sake of him who loves us, a love that does not demand reciprocation, a love that endures even when its object is unlovely, a love that enables us to say to all those who find it hard to love or whom nobody seems to love, "His peace be with you."

1 JOHN 5:20

And we know that the Son of God has come
and has given us understanding,
to know him who is true;
and we are in him who is true,
in his Son Jesus Christ.
This is the true God and eternal life.

PRAYER

Although the world may be in the power of evil, Lord,
I abide safely in you.
Although things happen that I simply cannot understand,
I will walk with you,
until that time when I walk with you always,
and there is no darkness nor shadow of death
in that bright land where the Lord reigns in glory.

FORTY
WHO DO YOU SAY THAT I AM?

THE CALL

Picture the following scene in the ancient world. John the Baptist, a strong, virile man who lives in the wilderness and dresses in the skins of wild animals wanders the Judean countryside, proclaiming that Christ, the Redeemer and Deliverer, is at hand. John is a man of God, the last of the prophets and the forerunner of Christ. Echoing the words of Isaiah, he proclaims, "I am the voice of one crying in the wilderness, 'Make straight the way of the Lord' " (John 1:23).

His voice drums across the arid wastes of a spiritual wilderness.

If you have traveled in a desert, you know how easy it is to lose your sense of direction. The land spreads out ceaselessly before you. No markers tell you where you are. The heat rises from the land with such intensity that the human eye cannot see accurately. The horizon shimmers and slides. Mirages warp and twist everything. You can be certain of nothing.

In many respects, the Jewish kingdom prior to John's coming had become a spiritual wilderness. The people had awaited the Messiah so long they had lost a sense of direction. In their desert, they had set up many false signs. They created elaborate sets of rules. Everything had become mere ritual and formula—silent, dry, sterile. Life was a puzzle, a maze in the desert.

In the psychology departments of many colleges, you will find little boxes in which rats are trained. By pressing a lever a certain number of times, a rat can learn to receive his reward of a few pellets of food. Similarly, the Jews hoped they would receive a reward for keeping their rituals. They had dozens of laws governing the observance of the Sabbath alone. By being good, they thought they could *make* the Messiah come. And in the midst of this wilderness, John cried, Make straight the way of the Lord.

In the ancient world, the major thoroughfare was called the King's Highway, just as U.S. 80 is called a federal highway. The King's Highway had to be kept straight, free of potholes and detours. It was the main thoroughfare, a road all people could follow.

John saw people wandering in a spiritual wilderness, and he called to them, The King is coming! Mend the road. Fill the potholes. Prepare to meet him. The Messiah, King of Kings, is on the way. In this desert of mazes, of twisting and turning, of mirages and false hopes, John proclaimed that it was time to straighten out one's life.

As he was preaching his message and baptizing people in the Jordan River, Jesus appeared. Immediately, John recognizes his King, his Lord, and pays homage to him.

"Behold," says John, "the Lamb of God, who takes away the sin of the world" (John 1:29). This is the one of whom I spoke. Here is the Messiah.

THE CHOICE

The next day, Jesus calls his first disciples—Andrew, Peter, and then Philip. The word is spreading. The Messiah is at hand. Philip immediately rushes out to recruit others.

Belief in God is an infectious thing, and one standard by which to evaluate our own relationship with Jesus is whether we have told others the good news that the King has come.

Philip finds Nathanael and tells him the Messiah has arrived. Now the first three disciples had seen Jesus face-to-face. Nathanael must accept Philip's word for it. This is the frustrating reality of witnessing. Unless the Holy Spirit works to reveal Christ to the other person, our efforts fall on deaf ears. Notice what Philip says: The Messiah, the one foretold by the patriarch Moses, has come, and he is Jesus of Nazareth, the son of Joseph (John 1:45).

Oh, at least let it be Jesus of Hebron or Joppa or some great city, Nathanael must have thought. Let it be Jesus of Washington, D.C., son of the senator. Let it be Jesus of Philadelphia, son of the millionaire. But Jesus of Nazareth? I imagine Nathanael almost laughed as he said, "Can anything good come out of Nazareth?" (John 1:46).

Nazareth, you see, was a small village, a farming community. It was located a couple of miles from the larger city of Japhia, which was the strongest fortress in lower Galilee at the time. Nazareth was a little outpost of the main camp. The name Nazareth, in fact, means "guardplace."

Nazareth, though, shared none of the glory of the larger Japhia. It was a town of farmers who tilled the nearby hillside. It was far from any trade route, removed from any larger city. The very reason Nazareth came into being was because a spring had its source under the city, making fresh water abundant for farmers and neighboring residents.

Jesus visited his city once during his ministry. Apparently, he worked miracles of healing there. Apparently, too, he called the people to repentance. In the very heart of staid tradition, in the synagogue itself, Jesus told the people to change their ways. We know this man, said the people; he grew up right next to us. He was Joseph the carpenter's son. Who does he think he is to be acting like God?

Can any good come out of Nazareth?

It strikes me that we often ask this question of our own lives. Frequently, we think we are not worthy of serving the Lord. We get weighed down by the troubles of the day—by the finances and unpaid bills that lurk on the table like a monster. Or by the alcoholism that began years ago with a few drinks and now taunts us every night. Or by the marriage that once seemed as sweet as a summer morning and now is so bitter that partners hardly speak to each other. Can any good come out of the narrow, little paths of our lives? It can come only when we recognize the Giver of life and acknowledge him as King.

You see, when they brought Jesus out to Calvary to crucify him, it was more than a crucifixion. They had stripped him. They had spat upon his head where the blood still was ugly and wet from the thorns. They had beaten him with whips that were braided together with jagged bits of iron. The soldiers had led him around from cells to various judges. He had eaten prison fare of moldy bread and a chunk of rotten fish with maggots in it.

After all this, they took Jesus to Calvary. Never was there a man who looked less like a king. And they placed a sign at the top of his cross: Jesus of Nazareth, King of the Jews. This man, this poor fool from Nazareth, thought he was king. Some people said to Pilate, the sign should really say that he *claimed* he was King of the Jews. Let it stand, said Pilate. Let's get it over with. Jesus of Nazareth. King? It is too foolish to consider.

Is this what comes out of Nazareth? A lonely, ugly death at the end of a long road? A man of thirty-three or so, a confused carpenter's son who claimed to be the Messiah?

Two others hung side by side with Jesus. One man had closely watched him. He had seen the mockery, the beatings, the brutality. The man was a thief and probably had been sentenced to die as a lesson to the people. He hung on the cross to Jesus' right.

On the cross to Jesus' left hung another man—also a thief, perhaps a murderer. He went into eternity defiantly jeering at Jesus. Caught by the spirit of the mob, he mocked the King from Nazareth even as he died.

But the man on the right—the man whose life may have been wasted by greed, by immorality, by selfishness—saw eternity before him in his dying minutes and appealed to the only King who can ever save man from what he is: Jesus of Nazareth. The thief repented. He changed. He recognized that Jesus is Lord. And Jesus of Nazareth gave to him the kingdom of heaven. "Today," Jesus said, "you will be with me in Paradise" (Luke 23:43).

Here was a man, a common low thief who we might say was no good, who may as well die, whose life was a waste, who had thrown away everything, who we would say was set straight for hell. And Jesus called him home to heaven. Why? Because he believed that Jesus was King.

In a sense we all hang to the right or the left of the Cross. Even now we take our positions. Do we go down through eternity jeering him as the man who would be king? Or do we confess that he is Lord of all?

Can any good come out of Nazareth?

THE FINAL ACT
On the cross, Jesus uttered few words, but they were words that emerged out of his deepest human need. "I thirst" (John 19:28). The King who created heaven and earth, the seas, and all that is in them, thirsted. Words of deep anguish and love for Mary: "Woman, behold, your son" (John 19:26). And to the disciple, "Behold, your mother" (John 19:27). The One who told us to love one another was dying before his mother's eyes. Those who

loved him best were helpless. Of the words of Jesus, however, none seem to be more anguished—yet more beautiful—than the simple phrase: "It is finished" (John 19:30).

Those might well be both the most agonized words and the most glorious words in all of history. For the man from Nazareth, a life of pain and struggle was finished. A life of misunderstanding, often accompanied by hatred, was ended. I remember awakening one morning in 1968 and turning on the 7:00 A.M. news. Bobby Kennedy had been killed just hours before. When I snapped on the television, I saw a film clip of a screaming mob and the slain body in the hotel lobby. The commentator closed the clip with these words: "Robert Kennedy, who fought for peace, now is at peace."

For Jesus, the human struggle drew to a close at Calvary. It was finished. But if we leave Golgotha with this view only, we have no Easter. For Jesus' final words point ahead. His earthly ministry ended so that a new and glorious ministry could begin. His death would bring perfect peace.

You see, the words "It is finished" were also used to complete a legal transaction in Jesus' day. When a bargain had been made, the goods delivered, and the *full price paid,* the transaction would be signed: It is finished. In our age we would stamp that bill: Paid in full. When a bill is paid in full, the slate is wiped clean and a new account begins.

On the cross, Jesus cried, It is finished. Your sins are paid in full. Will you stop your worry, your struggle, your tears? I cried for you. I shed my blood for you. I, Jesus, the Son of God, have conquered for you. The debt is paid.

When you tote up all the sins of a lifetime on a very large blackboard, Jesus reaches down from the cross and wipes that blackboard clean with his nail-pierced hand. My son, my daughter, he says, it is finished. When that happens—and only then—can we find a fresh start.

When we meet the risen Christ, the old life is finished and the joy is just beginning. There is comfort for our darkest hour, love and light and boundless power. Freed from the guilt of transgression, we know that even as we turn our faces to Jesus and say, Father, forgive us, he says in return: It is finished. Come all ye who are weary and heavy laden. It is finished. I am the resurrection. I am the light. In me you shall find new lives.

By these words of Jesus, we claim our birthrights as sons and daughters of the most high King. We are worthy because we belong to him. Jesus has given us value. No more should we think of ourselves as poor, desperate sinners. That *is finished.*

Instead, we are joint heirs with Christ. If we have suffered with him, we shall also be glorified with him (Rom. 8:17). We are no longer servants, but people set free by the King himself.

We are given power. As heirs with Christ, we may call upon our Father and he will answer us (John 14:13, 14).

The fruits of the Spirit dwell in us. Fruits of faith, hope, love, and kindness flourish in our spirits (Gal. 5:22, 23).

The King has mighty warriors—legions of angels—and they are given charge over us (Matt. 4:6).

The King's dominion is established for peace, and his peace shall rule in our hearts (Col. 3:15). This is not a peace of our own making, but a peace the King gives to *rule* in our hearts. He will not let us be troubled.

But above all, the King from Nazareth calls us to be part of his kingdom for ever and ever. C. S. Lewis closes his *Chronicles of Narnia* with this magnificent vision of *that* kingdom:

The things that began to happen after that were so great and beautiful that I cannot write them. And for us this is the end of all the stories, and we can most truly say that they all lived happily ever after. But for them it was only the beginning of the real story. All their life in this world and all their adventures in Narnia had only been the cover and the title page: now at last they were beginning Chapter One of the Great Story, which no one on earth has read: which goes on for ever: in which every chapter is better than the one before.

Can any good come out of Nazareth?
And Jesus turned to the thief on his right and said, "Today you will be with me in Paradise."

DANIEL 4:3
His kingdom is an everlasting kingdom,
and his dominion is from generation to generation.

PRAYER
Lord, a familiar song affirms that
"Jesus shall reign where'er the sun
Does His successive journeys run;
His kingdom spread from shore to shore,
Till moons shall wax and wane no more."
Thine is the power,
and the glory,
and the kingdom forever. Amen.